PRACTICAL SHOOTER'S GUIDE

A How-To Approach for Unconventional Firing Positions and Training

Text Copyright © 2016 Sidewinder Industries

All Rights Reserved

A special thanks to Matt, Tyson, and Cory for their help with editing, and thank you to Mike and Joe for assisting with photography, along with everyone else involved. Couldn't have done it without you guys.

Table of Contents

Introduction 5
1 Brief Touch on Basic Fundamentals 8
   Trigger Control 8
   Sight Alignment/Sight Picture 9
   Breathing 13
   Body Positioning 14
2 Positional Principles 16
   Front Support 16
   Rear Support 21
   Get Low 22
   Support Hand 23
   Wind and Dialing 26
   Economy of Motion 31
3 Overview of Supported Positions 33
   Kneeling Positions 33
   Sitting Positions 38
   Standing Positions 41
   Slings 44
   Real World and Competition Position Comparisons ... 53
4 Bags and Backpacks 55
   Backpacks 57
5 Rooftops, Slopes, & Tank Traps 60

    Reverse Rooftops/Slopes 63

    Side Slopes 66

    Tank Traps 70

6 Tripods, Bipods, & Shooting Sticks 76

    Bipods & Shooting Sticks 79

7 Support-Side Shooting 81

8 Bolt Manipulation 84

9 Shot Procedures 93

10 Importance of Dry-Fire Practice 97

    Dry Fire Enablers 99

11 Training Regimen 102

    Round Counts & After Actions 104

    Time Limits and Physical Stressors 105

    Targets and Ranges 107

    Weather Considerations 108

    Video Recording 110

    Range Buddies 111

12 Standards & Time Trials 113

13 Rifle Precision 121

14 Firing Through Brush 126

    Test #1 128

    Test #2 131

    Practical Takeaways 134

15 Summary 137

    About the Author 139

Introduction

I started shooting competitively in long range when I was roughly 16 years old with my father. He shot NRA Service Rifle in his younger years and was influential in helping me learn the fundamentals of marksmanship as well as getting me involved in Service Rifle competitions. Shortly after I became involved in Service Rifle, I learned about another style of long-range shooting called practical precision rifle. This style of shooting was, and still is, predominantly run at smaller local matches but was rapidly growing in both exposure and popularity. These precision rifle matches were so vastly different from anything else going on due to the difficult and engaging elements to them, which made it something I was very excited to be a part of.

Precision rifle matches had been going on for years before I got involved with them (2008-2009 timeframe), but were still what I would consider a fledgling movement. Having 15-20 shooters at a local monthly match was considered an incredible turnout. The COF (Course of Fire) was structured differently than it is today; stages involved mostly prone shooting positions, and one could always expect a hostage stage or two. Some things have remained the same throughout the years as hostage stages still show up occasionally. Certain stages such as KYL (Know Your Limitations), and "Crazy Steel" (targets at a variety of ranges engaged as quickly as possible) are still found in matches today.

Positional shooting mainly consisted of a slung stage, rooftop stage, or the occasional simple barricade. Positional stages and shooting at reactive steel targets were what made it fun. However, not many people put in dedicated time to practice weird barricades and alternative positions (I did not anyway) to become fully acquainted with their gear. One could usually place very well in the match depending only on their prone shooting skills.

Gear selection was very limited. For optics, new shooters were recommended to get the Leupold Mk 4, Nightforce, or U.S. Optics scopes with the vast majority sporting simple Mil-Dot SFP (Second Focal Plane) reticles and MOA turrets (minute of angle). As for rifles, Remington 700 actions dominated the firing lines. Custom actions were rare, and if there was one on the line, everybody had to come check it out. If someone wanted to upgrade their stock, the HS Precision or Accuracy International 1.5/2.0 chassis were the go-to options. Caliber selection consisted mostly of .308s with a few .260s thrown in. Consumers had relatively few options to choose from for upgrading their rifles.

Today, we all enjoy a broad selection of optics, stocks, actions, and a variety of other rifle accessories to fit our needs. This change is due largely in part to the rise in popularity of this shooting style, and shooters are voicing their concerns and desires to help drive product development forward. Shooters began having a better understanding of what was needed to increase their hit percentages as skill levels increased and COFs grew more complicated.

It has been exciting to watch the dramatic rise of the general population's shooting skills, especially in matches. Typically there were about 2-3 guys that would always dominate any match they attended. That still exists but to a lesser degree. It is nearly impossible to show up to a match with no practice beforehand and walk away with the match win. The skill level and dedication that shooters today are putting into the sport have eclipsed those of previous years.

I believe the largest factor in the improvement of the average shooter isn't necessarily all the gear; it's the way the shooter approaches obstacles and how they properly train for them. Barricades and completely new positions are often approached with a feeling of anxiety for newer shooters, or shooters who are not practiced in this style of shooting. Shooters are now approaching these new positions by building barricades and other contraptions in their backyards to conduct dry fire practice, or to bring to the range.

The way that I approach positional shooting and training is vastly different than what I did seven years ago. I mostly shot from my belly, and most of the "practice" I did was during live fire. Dry fire has worked wonders for my training regimen and is a staple in most other successful shooters training as well. It builds a knowledge base from which shooters can draw for future obstacles that are encountered. Instead of approaching shooting obstacles with uncertainty, shooters now come at them head first with confidence.

Everyone has their way of doing things, and this is especially true in the shooting world. The topics outlined in the following chapters present how I have approached my shooting in recent years. My approach has been helpful for me, but that doesn't mean other methods won't also bring you success. The following chapters will show you how I do certain things, but also explain **why** I made the choice to do something since that aspect seems to be an overlooked part of breaking down and explaining different shooting positions.

My goal for you as the reader is to leave with an understanding of different positions and why they work, how to improve your positional shooting, and gain the knowledge to accurately predict what position you will use when approaching an obstacle whether it be in a competition or hunting in the mountains.

1 Brief Touch on Basic Fundamentals

I won't take too long on this topic, as there are multiple books, YouTube videos, DVD's, etc., which cover this in depth. If you are a brand new shooter, I would highly recommend getting personal instruction on this as it will serve you much better than any video. Attempting many types of positional shooting will only serve to frustrate the shooter if the fundamentals are not at least familiar and somewhat mastered.

Trigger Control

While all of the fundamentals are important, I consider trigger control to be especially crucial. The squeezing of the trigger is the last conscious input that you transmit to the rifle. After that, recoil takes its path, and you reap the reward, or penalty, of your body position. It's such a small movement, but making a bad trigger press can send shots wildly off target, especially when firing from an unstable position.

There will always be some amount of wobble when shooting in positions other than prone, and timing the shot to go off when the reticle is within the target is difficult to accomplish when poor trigger techniques are employed. The most common I have seen is "slapping" the trigger. The finger is usually hovering off the trigger, and when the shooter determines that NOW is the time to fire, they quickly pull their finger to the rear and "slap" the trigger. There is a saying in shooting that rings true, and it is that "consistency is accuracy." Slapping the trigger is anything but consistent. The finger never pulls the trigger in the same place and often provokes a sympathetic contraction of the rest of the muscles in the hand, which results in unwanted movement before the bullet exits the muzzle.

The trigger should lie a flat 90 degrees to the finger and somewhere in the middle of the tip of the finger and the first knuckle. Pulling straight back lends itself to a consistent pull with no lateral movement or uneven forces exerted upon the trigger. Uneven pressure on either side of the trigger will shift the impact of the bullet. Reason being that if you are pressing on the side of the trigger, the force is not being evenly distributed. Once recoil (energy) begins, it will always follow the path of least resistance. Since there is less pressure on the opposite side you are squeezing, the rifle will want to move in that direction, instead of straight back.

Sight Alignment/Sight Picture

When dealing with magnified optics, sight alignment is *ensuring there is perfect edge-to-edge clarity in the field of view with no shadowing around the edges*. Sight picture is *adjusting the image to be completely parallax-free*. Parallax is the apparent movement of the reticle in relation to the target as perceived by the eye.

Obviously, this is something that we want to eliminate since consistent shot placement is difficult to achieve if the reticle is in a slightly different location every time. Other factors also play into the amount of perceived parallax.

The level of magnification the scope is on plays a large factor in how easily it is to obtain proper sight picture and sight alignment. Often times, choosing to run a medium level of magnification (10-15 power) is advantageous. Magnification between 10x-15x widens the field of view and reduces (or eliminates) the parallax error found when viewing targets at different ranges. The higher the magnification, the smaller the exit pupil of the optic becomes. As a result, the sight picture and parallax become less forgiving to small errors in head placement.

Parallax is by far the most overlooked aspect of long-range shooting. If our focal planes are not aligned correctly, our rifles are pointed in slightly different locations for every shot despite the reticle appearing to be in the center of the target. The distances being shot play into this as well. The parallax error between 100 yards and 500 yards is, or should be, very obvious by the "fuzziness" of the image. However, the parallax error between 600 yards and 1000 yards is much less.

If we think about the error in terms of the relative distance changes, it makes more sense. The 500-yard shot is five times further compared to the 100-yard shot, whereas the 1000-yard shot is only about 1.67 times further than 600 yards. The latter distances have much less difference in overall parallax adjustment. Depending on the optic and magnification setting, this difference may not even be noticeable.

Sometimes we won't have time to adjust the parallax properly. The balance between magnification, parallax, and target size needs to be weighed for each situation. Let's say I needed to engage a 3-4 MOA target at 200 yards and then a 1.5 MOA target at 600 yards immediately after that. I would set my parallax to be correct around 600 yards and power my scope down around 8x-10x to engage the larger 200-yard target. I would do this because the closer target is much larger and backing the magnification down relieves a lot of the parallax error. Once the closer target has been engaged and I'm moving to the longer shot, I could increase my magnification and already have the parallax correct.

If I have the time and am shooting at one range or a few ranges that are very close to each other, I will dial in the parallax as perfectly as possible. Disregard the yardage markings found on the parallax knobs that most scopes have. Differences in diopter settings, atmospherics, and prescriptions will cause these settings to vary. Use the distance markings as reference points for the correct parallax adjustment, such as if my correct parallax setting for 100 yards is actually around the 150-yard marker on the knob. Crank the magnification all the way up to max power to make the parallax more "picky". Maximum magnification ensures that you will get the adjustment as correct as possible. When you bring the magnification back down, you know for certain that you have nothing to worry about with your parallax.

Having the stock and cheek piece properly adjusted plays a large part in maintaining proper head position, which is something I believe a lot of shooters do not take the time to examine. I like to be able to relax my head completely on the cheek piece and be able to see perfectly through the optic. Not relaxing down into the rifle forces more muscles in the neck to be used than is necessary. This becomes more prevalent as soon as positions other than prone are encountered. Once the position becomes more unstable it is easier to miss the smaller details such as having proper sight alignment. If the gear is fit properly to the body, this helps reduce the chance of errors in sight alignment.

Observe below the edge-to-edge clarity, indicating proper sight alignment.

Improper sight alignment visible by the "scope shadowing" in the bottom right-hand side.

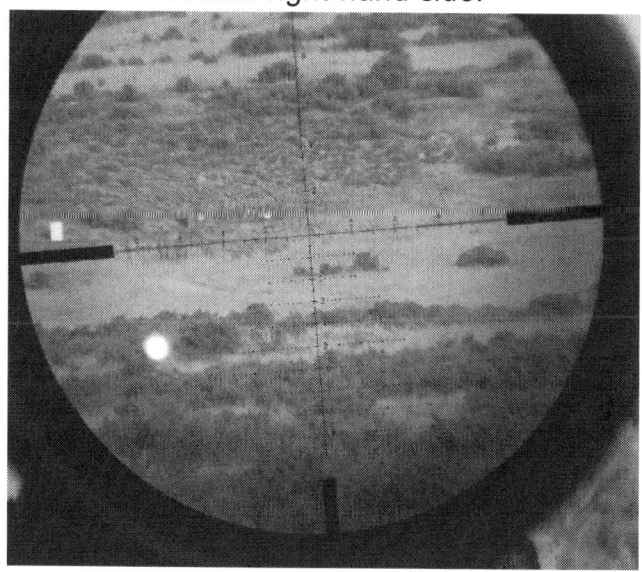

Breathing

As I am sure you have heard by now, the "sweet spot" in the breathing cycle is the natural respiratory pause (bottom of the breathing cycle). There are a couple of reasons for this. The first reason being that it is the most relaxed and consistent point in the breathing cycle. If the breath is being held at the very top or bottom of the cycle, the diaphragm is forced to do additional work to hold the excess air in, or contract and remain contracted to push past that natural resting point. Again, if we can relax as many muscles as possible, do so.

Breathing also has a slight effect on the heart rate through what is called respiratory sinus arrhythmia. This phenomenon is the slight quickening of the heart rate during inhalation and slight decreasing of the heart rate during exhalation. The next time you lay down to bed or are hooked up to a heart rate monitor, try exhaling very slowly and notice your heart rate compared to when you inhale. For me, I notice heartbeat in the reticle when shooting from different positions. No matter what I do, it's almost always there. The effects of heart rate vary amongst shooters and their physiology, placement of arteries in their body, etc. You either do or do not notice it. So since I do notice it, I find prolonging my exhale to let my heart rate slow down just a touch to be beneficial.

Prolonging my exhale as I am getting into position also serves as a mental reminder to pump the brakes if I'm feeling rushed. If we are on the clock, we often find ourselves hurrying through tasks and having a feeling of urgency. Taking a big breath or two and slowly letting it out as I am getting into position helps bring me back to what is important; getting a solid position and breaking good shots.

Body Positioning

There are many good sources of information out there on how to properly lay behind the rifle these days. Multiple DVD's and online tutorials go over how and why we want to square our shoulders and lay straight behind the rifle to maximize recoil management for follow up shots. However, the best place to learn is in person through a class. In positional shooting, getting the shoulders square to the rifle is not always possible, or the best choice to maximize stabilization for the position. Situation dictates, but we still want to get as much meat as possible behind the rifle to absorb recoil. Being able to spot your impacts (or more importantly, your misses) is crucial to shooting from alternative positions. If you lose the target after recoil and the bullet missed, you have no way of accurately adjusting your rounds.

A spotter will not always be around to call corrections in a match or while hunting on the mountain. With the vast majority of competition shooters having switched over to various 6mm/6.5mm cartridges, controlling recoil is not as pronounced of a problem in a match setting as it used to be when .308 was the norm. The addition of muzzle brakes and suppressors only add to this benefit.

Once you start venturing into the heavier recoiling calibers, recoil is just going to be a burden that you have to bear when firing from a position other than prone. Powering down the optic is the easiest and the best way to combat recoil and maintain a good sight picture after good body positioning. However, there isn't any hope of maintaining a decent sight picture of the impact area with heavier calibers if the rifle is built around a poor body position.

2 Positional Principles

The three fundamental things to look for when approaching shooting obstacles are:

1 - Find solid support for the front of the rifle.

2 - Utilize any rear support when possible for the rifle and/or firing elbow.

3 - Getting your body and rifle as low to the ground/support as is comfortable.

Obviously, the situation will dictate the specifics of the shot, but these three things are essential to providing a steady position.

Front Support

Having something to support the front of the rifle is the first fundamental of positional shooting. A solid front support goes hand in hand with knowing where to place the rifle on that support. What I see most often is shooters jamming the magazine, or magazine well, against the edge of whatever they are shooting from. There are a few reasons that I prefer not to use this technique for **most** situations. The first of which being that the fulcrum, or pivot point, is placed nearly directly in the middle of the rifle. Any movement at the rear of the rifle results in an equal, or sometimes increased amount of movement at the muzzle. If the fulcrum is shifted as far forward as the shooter can comfortably reach on the stock, this usually translates to less overall movement at the muzzle. Resting on the forward portion of the stock, rather than the middle, reduces the amount of large wobbles off target. Note that this is the technique that works best for me, and that there are many shooters who balance the rifle in the middle quite well.

There are situations where that may not be the best option, as no single technique is a one size fits all, so keep that in mind. I've found (for me and my rifle) that if the forward surface of the rifle is supported by is roughly 3"-4" or more in thickness, then it can be more advantageous to use a small front bag in between the supporting surface and the stock. Using a small bag on the front helps deaden some of the "jump" of the rifle on hard surfaces and maximizes the surface area the stock is in contact with. This is where extra stability can be obtained, with the maximization of surface areas and points of contact.

The other reason that I (generally) prefer not to jam the magazine is when the position does not have an open top (barricade hole/small window). The shooter is then forced to try and thread the rifle through the opening. Scopes, scope caps and bipods often hinder this movement and drain precious seconds. Placing only the front portion of the rifle stock through requires much less movement and results in nearly zero adjustments needed in and out of different positions since the bipod can act as a barrier stop.

Take a look at the photo below. Bipods and scopes will get in the way while attempting to thread them through the holes.

If you can't quickly adjust the fore and aft placement of your bipod and don't have enough room on your stock in front to rest upon, this can be easily remedied by running one of the bipod legs up/forward and leaving the other down. The forward leg serves as a resting point for the front, while the other leg that is down serves as the stop that affords some forward loading to help with recoil absorption. Both bipod legs up also can provide a decent support if forward loading is not an option.

I'm fortunate enough to have a quick-adjust bipod system that uses picatinny rails. My default position is more towards the rear portion of the rail. This affords me enough area forward of the bipod to rest the stock on obstacles, as well as being close enough to reach with my support hand from the prone position. A small detail, but one that is often overlooked. I think everyone can recall a time when the correct bipod height was misjudged and some adjustment was required. If the bipod is mounted all the way forward, it is often out of reach and forces the shooter to completely break position to adjust the legs (depending on the stock used and whether or not you have gorilla arms).

I picked up this nugget of knowledge from other members of the Deliberate Dynamics training cadre, and now keep the bipod legs within reach from the prone position without having to break my position or cheek weld behind the optic. This saves a substantial amount of time and helps get eyes back on target faster after the adjustment.

Below, you can see the height adjustment is just barely out of comfortable reach without breaking position. The following photos display the bipod adjusted a little further to the rear, resulting in a comfortable and quick bipod adjustment.

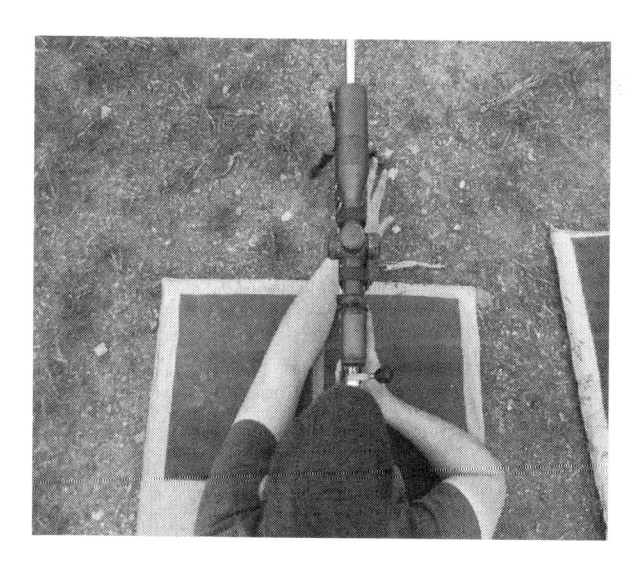

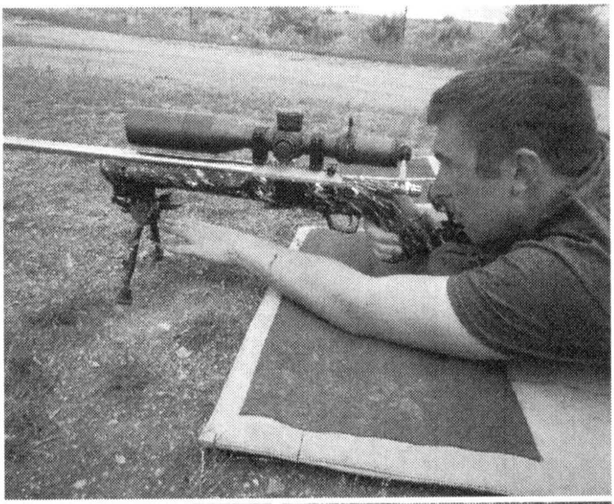
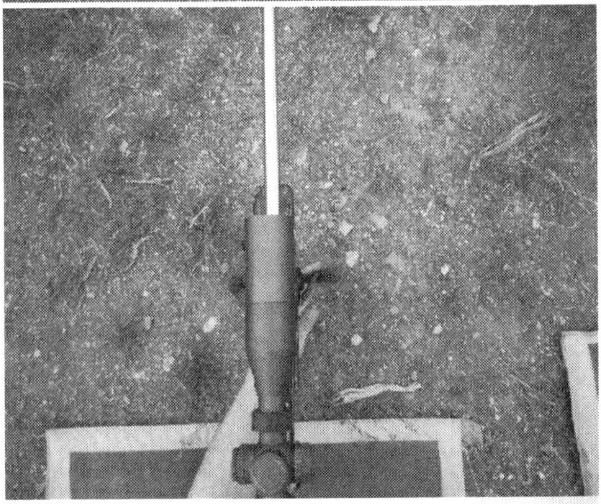
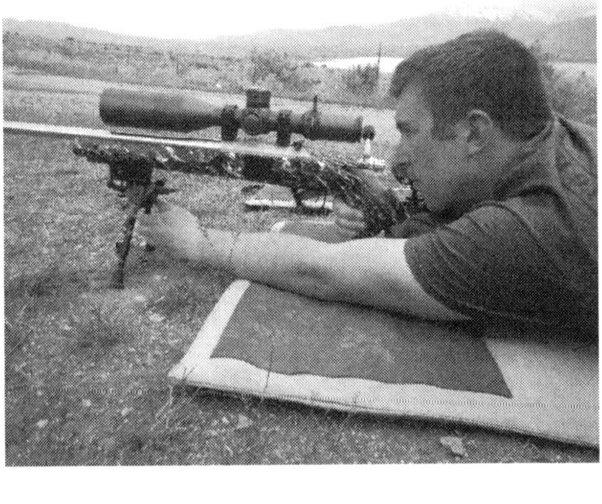

Rear Support

The second principle is finding optimal support for the rear of the rifle. Being able to support the rear of the rifle with either a piece of gear or another body part that is anchored, will help to drastically reduce the wobble area. When new shooters (or shooters that are just now to positional shooting) are trying to figure out positional shooting, I often observe the support arm reaching back to the buttstock in an attempt to provide additional stability. This does not work to assist in stabilizing the rear of the rifle at all.

The reason being is that when making adjustments from prone, that entire support arm, elbow, and bag are anchored to the ground, a solid base. This enables steady adjustments to be made to the rifle. Once the shooter is up and off the belly, the only thing that rear arm remains in contact with is the torso...which is also waving around up in the air, not anchored to anything stable.

The ultimate goal is a medium that is sturdy enough to support the rifle and reduce wobble area. If supporting the buttstock is not possible, the next best thing is getting the firing-side elbow supported. This can be done with the side of a fence, with a knee, a backpack, etc. Getting the front and rear of the rifle supported as best as possible will provide the least amount of wobble area in the position. Having less wobble area translates to a higher percentage of time that the reticle is within the target's edges which should, in turn, increase the hit percentage. I think that is something we can all get behind, right?

Examples of different rear supports will be addressed later including bags, backpacks, tripods, shooting sticks, and the most advantageous body positions for each of these supports.

Get Low

Finally, the third principle is to get low. As you are building your position, see if there are ways to get the rifle and your body as low to the ground as is comfortable. Typically, the closer to the ground you are, the more stable you will be. Situation dictates, of course, since there are a variety of factors to consider such as the shooter's flexibility, gear used, previous injuries, and the height of the obstacle. Typically, getting lower to the ground will create smaller gaps that need to be filled to assist in steadying the rifle.

For example, take note of how stable your high-kneeling position is compared to a regular, lower kneeling position. Even if you can get the firing elbow supported in the high-kneeling position (which is ideal) your center of gravity is now much higher, and your legs are spread out much further. The hip stabilizers must now constantly be working to keep your torso upright, and this shows through increased horizontal wobbles of the reticle. This will be touched on again with pictures showing the difference in the "Kneeling Positions" section. If a backpack or large bag can fill the gap between the buttstock and the knee, mashing down into that helps eliminate a lot of the additional horizontal wobble area.

The lower kneeling position does not activate as many small muscles that quickly tire. Shooters can usually sink right into a low kneeling with ease (barring injuries). The gap between the knee and elbow/buttstock is minimal and can be easily filled with a pack or bag. A lower position of any kind will almost always win out compared to a higher one.

If the shooter has injuries that prevent being able to build certain positions, then alternative positions must be sought. Knee pads can help ease the stress on the knees, especially when kneeling on hard surfaces. Some shooters find less stress if they put both knees down, rather than only one, since the weight is more evenly distributed. This eliminates a shelf for the firing elbow and rifle, but I routinely see shooters do very well from the double-kneeling position.

In addition to getting lower to the ground, shooters should also look for opportunities to lean/relax their body against walls or other supports. Leaning against the side of a wall in any elevated position will help a lot of muscles to relax, making the position more stable. Leaning against and being supported by a structure also aids in resisting the effects of the wind on the body. During blustery days, problems shooting from different positions are compounded by gusts of wind blowing both our bullets and positions around.

Support Hand

While this isn't necessarily one of my three positional principles, the support hand does play an important role in different positions. I've found that it's usually best practice to run the hand forward to where the stock and obstacle meet unless an alternative rear support is being used such as a tripod. Placing the hand forward can aid in keeping some of the recoil and muzzle rise in check. If the obstacle doesn't grip the rifle's stock effectively, or there isn't much surface area, reaching forward on the stock can also help keep the rifle from recoiling out of position.

I also might apply a slight push into the barricade (if the obstacle allows), while slightly pulling the rifle into my shoulder with my fingers. I am not forcefully pushing into the rifle and barricade; it is more of a gentle lean. Leaning requires little muscle activation and your body weight aids in managing recoil forces. Gripping forward can also aid in reducing the wobble area (this can be largely shooter dependent).

The support hand is providing a small amount of rearward force while keeping the stock anchored on an unstable obstacle.

The improvement I have noticed while applying some rearward force is a reduction in larger wobbles off the target area, resulting in more time that the reticle is actually within the target area. The amount of pulling with the support hand does vary depending on the rifle/barricade and will obviously vary amongst different shooters with what works best. Keep in mind that the amount of "pull" required is minimal. Personally, this isn't much more force than what the tips of my fingers can curl in.

In other positions where the rifle may be placed further in on the obstacle, and the obstacle has sidewalls, pressing the side of the rifle or optic into the obstacle can be advantageous. This maximizes the amount of surface area the rifle has with the barrier and helps to eliminate some of the potential wobbles. As a general rule, the more surface area of the rifle that is in contact with the barrier, the more stable and consistent you will be. The rifle also locks into place by being pinned with the support arm or hand to the side and bottom of the obstacle.

Pinning the stock into the corner with my support hand.

Wind and Dialing

First off, let me state that this section will not be going into painstaking detail over reading the wind. There are entire books written on the subject by shooters who are much more qualified than I on this topic. What I will say is this, making an accurate and quick second-round adjustment is much more beneficial than taking forever trying to read every detail of the wind, only to have it change by the time you've made up your mind.

While wind formulas can be fun, I find they often cause unneeded confusion, especially in newer shooters that are still trying to figure this game out. There are many other options for referencing the wind that are more simple and practical in their use and execution. I'm sure this will rile a good portion of you up, but I have never found much use for the wind formulas personally. If you shoot enough of the same caliber, the wind values often become somewhat memorized. Wind values for a set direction and speed, such as full-value for 5 or 10 mph, can be easily memorized for quick benchmark ranges such as 400, 700, and 1000 yards. For in-between ranges, this becomes a quick estimation, but wind values don't change nearly as drastically as elevation does between yard lines.

Almost everyone has a ballistic solver with them these days, and if you don't, then I highly recommend acquiring one. Whether on a cell phone or a Kestrel, the wind calculation produced will be more accurate than using a rough formula you have to work through in your head. For those situations where time is of the essence or electronics are not an option, recording a full-value wind reference such as 10 mph, or 5 mph is the most practical alternative. The wind values are best recorded right next to the corresponding elevation data for each distance.

A data card with both elevation and 10 mph full-value wind holds for quick reference

The most important aspect of shooting in the wind is spotting where the round impacted to determine future actions. If the round missed, take the extra second to see exactly where that miss lines up on the reticle relative to your original aiming point. That spot in the reticle where the round impacted is now your new aiming point, so make the correct adjustment before the wind changes! All the care in the world can be put into reading the wind and using formulas to make that perfect first-round impact (which is what we want!), but a lot of the time this doesn't happen at longer ranges. If you can't effectively spot the miss and accurately adjust, you're just wasting rounds.

In almost all cases, making windage adjustments by holding the scope's reticle off the target (assuming a first focal plane optic is in use) will be the most practical solution. Wind holds provide the fastest solution to put rounds on target and eliminate any confusion experienced in dialing turrets. However, this can sometimes be less precise when firing from an unsupported and uncomfortable position at smaller targets. Unless the wind happens to align with one of the stadia as a reference, you can sometimes be left holding on the target without a good point of reference in the scope's reticle. For larger targets, this isn't as much of a problem.

Another important aspect is to make your adjustments to the **center** of the target. Not making adjustments to the target's center is probably the most common mistake found with adjusting rounds on target, after giving corrections in inches (always give/make corrections in angular units of measurement, not linear! i.e. MOA/MIL = good, inches/feet = bad). Adjustments to the edge of the target only get you hits some of the time and waste rounds. Again, be sure to make your adjustments to the center of the target.

If the round impacts the target, take note of exactly where that round landed, if possible. If hanging steel targets are being shot, observe which direction the target spins or if it does at all. Hits closer to the edge will obviously spin the target in that direction. This should tell you to either increase or decrease your wind hold to bring impacts closer to the center. A center hit on a hanging target will have little to no left or right movement, mostly straight back. Use target feedback as much as possible to get a handle on the wind.

I've started to dial in my wind, or at least a portion of the wind, to more closely align the center of the reticle with the point of impact. This is only dealing with targets that are at a single range, or ranges that are close enough together that the wind call is relatively the same. I do this because our eyes are naturally drawn to the center of the reticle by default. Dialing the wind lets the eye naturally fall to the center and even if the wind call is incorrect, I have that much less to hold off the target and can reference easier. I also have a more definite aiming point than I would with holding in between hash marks. Note that this is done in a fairly relaxed environment where multiple targets at varying distances are not being engaged.

The caveat to manually adjusting windage is being painfully aware of which way the windage knob has been turned and remembering to set it back to zero once shooting has ceased. I always say in my head to "push left" and "pull right," meaning that when I rotate (push) the turret away (thumb moving forward) that it will shift the impact of the bullet left, or "push" it left. When I "pull" the turret, it will shift the impact of the bullet to the right. This only works for U.S. based scopes; European scopes often have their turrets turn in the opposite direction.

"Pushing" my thumb away/forward to adjust impacts left.

"Pulling" thumb back towards me to adjust impacts right.

Nevertheless, anytime you adjust that windage knob it should be a thorn in your side that nags until you bring the knob back to zero. Nothing is worse than watching a shooter get confused and frustrated as to why their impacts are way off to the left or right when they just forgot to dial the windage turret back to zero from a previous engagement. Practice and get comfortable using only holds for wind, then try some limited dialing.

A practice that I am adamant about that eliminates all dialing problems is simply checking my turrets before each stage or before I'm about to take an important shot outside of a match. It doesn't matter if you make a conscious effort to dial the turrets back to zero after every engagement unless you are always shooting at whatever yard line you are zeroed at. Your next shot at any other range will still be a miss if your turret is on zero. So check them before you shoot.

One exception would be when your turrets don't have a revolution indicator; in that case, I would recommend dialing back to your zero stop (or zero marker) after each engagement to avoid being a full revolution off. So make it a habit to be constantly checking your turrets before you are about to take a shot, or are approaching a stage. This will ensure the windage will always be where it needs to be, and the correct elevation will always be dialed.

Economy of Motion

By far, the largest amount of a shooter's wasted time is spent trying to get into the right position for a shot. Effective position prediction is essential to eliminating wasted time. If one or two different positions are already known to work for a specific height range or type of obstacle, you immediately fall into them instead of trying to figure out how to contort your legs and arms to gain the most stability.

This applies to getting out of the position as much as it does getting into it. Often times, you won't shoot from just a single position; you will be forced to move to different positions, and time wasted building and breaking each one accumulates quickly. Therefore, repeated practice in building, breaking, and moving to different positions should be a regular part of any practice and training sessions that occur.

Knowing which foot you are first going to step with for a seated position, or which way you will cross your legs as you sit can save a lot of time and frustration. I have seen this happen countless times; shooters will stutter-step into a sitting position and try to decide between crossing their legs a certain way, then decide to go to an open-legged sitting position after all that time and energy has been wasted.

Knowing where to place the gear that is used will cut back on time spent trying to make it work for you, as well as stay out of the way when not needed. Take/use only the gear you know will be useful to make the present shot. This simplifies the process of getting in and out of position and makes it less likely to fiddle with unnecessary gear that ends up doing nothing for you. Practice deploying and stowing the gear you plan on using for whatever activities you participate in. This breeds familiarity and lessens the chances of you fumbling with getting your gear into uncomfortable positions.

In general, I suggest supporting the front of the rifle before, or as you begin building a position. The largest reason for this is safety. If a barrier is already supporting the majority of the rifle's weight, the muzzle is much more likely to be pointed in a safe direction. This also frees up the other hand, and mind, to focus on positioning the gear and body in the best place possible.

3 Overview of Supported Positions

Kneeling Positions

Kneeling positions of varying heights are typically the most common position encountered when shooting from barricades or alternative support. Therefore, you should get comfortable in a broad range of kneeling positions and figure out what the limitations of your body are in those situations. In correlation with the 3rd general principle of trying to get as low to the ground as possible, this applies to both the rifle and the body. Lower kneeling positions should be relatively steady as long as the feet are kept under the hips/center of gravity. This gives solid support for the rest of the body and requires relatively few muscles to stabilize the position.

Any time that an obstacle supports the front of the rifle, and the shooter is in the kneeling position, the knee that is on the firing side should be up to provide a rest for the firing arm. If the position is low enough, the firing-side knee can even provide support for the buttstock of the rifle. When most people approach this position for the first time, their support-side knee is the one that is up, while the firing side knee is to the ground. This is just a habit that most of us have developed from firing rifles with a sling, or without any front support other than our arm.

Raising the wrong knee, leaving the firing-side elbow without support. Also shows an example of the support hand tucking the buttstock into the shoulder to unsuccessfully gain stability.

In those instances where we have nothing else to support the rifle with but our arms, that is absolutely the right way to go about it. But when firing from an obstacle, having the support-side knee up, rather than the firing-side knee, serves no purpose in aiding stabilization of the rifle. Using the firing-side knee for elbow or rifle support is much more effective, and can make a night-and-day difference in terms of stability.

As previously mentioned in the "Get Low" section, in the higher kneeling positions, the base is forced to open up by sliding the downed knee rearward which straightens the firing side shin to be perpendicular to the ground. This takes advantage of the full length of the shin to get as high as possible to support the elbow.

However, when the legs open up under the base, this activates more of the small stabilizing muscles in the hips and legs to maintain an upright posture. This results in an increased wobble area but is still preferable to the alternative awkward standing/bent over position with the torso nearly parallel to the ground. As mentioned before, using backpacks and large bags to help fill the gap between the elbow and the knee help immensely in assisting the stabilization of this position.

Here, I have my base spread out, forcing more muscles to activate to keep my balance.

This position below is much more relaxed, allowing me to focus on the more important factors of the shot.

Another issue I see quite often in kneeling positions is the pointing of the foot by the leg providing the rifle's support. Shooters tend to do this when their position is too low and need more elevation to acquire the target. The heel is raised and makes your calf muscle go into overtime trying to stabilize and support your body weight. Instead, the support-side knee should be brought straight back while the firing-side foot remains flat in the same place. This does open up your base some, but as I mentioned earlier, the position takes advantage of the full vertical length of your shin and shortens the gap between the knee and elbow in those higher kneeling positions. The benefits of getting the elbow, or buttstock, supported will outweigh the costs of opening up the base.

Pointing the foot while trying to gain needed elevation.

The straightened shin can provide elevation while remaining fairly stable.

Sitting Positions

I consider sitting positions a close 2nd to kneeling in the probability of being encountered. Thus, they should not be ignored. Flexibility will make or break you when it comes to seated positions. If you are a more flexible person, this will open up a variety of angles that you can position your legs and torso to gain stability. For this reason, I would highly recommend incorporating some regular stretching into your daily routine to reach some of these positions. Making time for stretching will go a long way to improving your level of comfort in shooting, as well as your day-to-day life.

Flexibility proves valuable in this position.

The sitting position should be a very stable option. We have a good, solid base on the ground that is very easy to relax into, as well as built-in rear support for the arms and rifle. Higher sitting positions may be less comfortable and will create larger empty spaces that need to be filled. A backpack, or large bag, make great tools to aid in supporting the rear of the rifle.

An example of a backpack being utilized in a higher sitting position.

Higher sitting positions may also be used for those barricade heights that are a little too short for a comfortable kneeling position by raising the knee and simply resting the rifle on the knee. This also allows for quick elevation adjustments by simply sliding the foot forward or back to change the height of the knee. A rear bag can also serve as a medium between the knee and rifle to help minimize any bounce from the recoil and aid in fine-tuning any elevation adjustments.

If possible, bringing the firing-side knee up and resting the foot against a rock or barricade can also help to improve the higher sitting positions. The leg remains stable enough to use as a rear support for the rifle or bag while the position remains fairly comfortable. However, this will lose effectiveness if nothing is available to brace the foot or leg and can contribute more to the wobble area.

Raised knee providing rear support for the rifle while the elbow provides some lateral support for the leg.

If the lower, more bent over sitting positions are not possible due to injuries or inflexibility, try using a double-kneeling position with a backpack positioned in front of the legs. The position's height will determine if the backpack, or bag, will be better suited on the ground or in the lap. One advantage this position has over a traditional cross-legged sitting position is increased mobility. The low double-kneeling position is easier to get in and out of in a pinch, compared to a regular sitting position. I would not suggest this position without some adequate rear support as the rear support makes a world of difference.

Double-kneeling position with a pack.

Standing Positions

For standing positions off obstacles, squaring the shoulders up behind the rifle is the most efficient way to absorb recoil. This is even more important in standing because you are high off the ground and often can't get as much body mass behind the rifle. Blading the shoulders to the rifle and barricade often accompanies running one leg far in front of the other. This weakens your base since there is little lateral stabilization or support, as well as activating large leg muscles that do not need to be doing as much work as they are. High winds can also move the shooter since, as stated above, there is no lateral support to resist it.

Below, the legs provide no lateral support and are not square to the rifle.

If the front support for the rifle is solid, the shooter should square up to the rifle with the shoulders and the feet, reduce any flex in the knees, and simply relax and lean forward into the rifle. Solid supports to lean against will not always be found, so slightly blading the shoulders may be required to keep the rifle in place through recoil.

Bent legs force quadriceps to support body weight.

Elevation adjustments are made by either bringing the feet closer together to raise the position, or spreading them further apart to get lower. Having the feet in line with each other and square to the rifle provides strong lateral support and enables as much relaxation as the position will allow without additional support. Combined with a forward lean, recoil becomes extremely manageable and excessive muzzle rise is minimized.

A forward lean with locked knees results in excellent recoil management and decent stability.

Slings

Slings have long been used to aid in the stabilization of different shooting positions. The more traditional practice of looping the arm through a cuff is still used today but is mostly found in NRA Palma and Service Rifle competitions. The cuff sling may also be used in other matches and few other scenarios, but these days the practice is largely a competition event since there is almost always alternative support in the area. Recent developments in sling use involve using a "patrol carry" fashion with the rifle slung across the body or clipping the rear portion of the sling into the belt.

While the traditional cuff sling isn't used as much as it was in the past, the increased stability can be useful in situations where there is little to no other option for supporting the rifle. For this reason, I still believe knowing how to employ a sling in all manners will serve to make you a well-rounded shooter.

To properly sling the rifle up, first, slip your support arm through the cuff. The style of cuff varies a great deal among different sling brands, but the function remains the same. The cuff will provide the best position if it is placed high up above the bicep. Having the cuff high up on the arm supports the weight of the rifle much better than if the cuff were placed closer to the elbow. This makes relaxing the support arm much easier.

A half twist is applied to the sling to provide a place for the hand to lie comfortably once the hand is wrapped around. If the sling is attached to the bottom of the stock, apply the half twist in a clockwise direction before looping the arm through. This is for right-handed shooters, reverse for lefties. If there are attachment points on both sides of your stock, placing the front portion of the sling on the right side, if you are right handed (left side if you are left handed), automatically puts the half twist in the sling.

Placing the sling cuff high on the arm. Observe the twist obtained by attaching the front of the sling to the side on the stock.

Once the hand is brought around the sling and in position on the stock, try to keep the rifle as close to directly over the elbow as possible. This helps the arm relax more muscles to aid in stabilization. If the arm is hanging out to the side, the position tires quickly and loses stability.

The hand is wrapped over the sling to provide tension and keep the rifle closer to the elbow.

Sling used with a bag to provide support in standing.

Using a sling to steady a position while the rifle is slung across the body is hardly new, but there are new slings released in recent years that specialize in this practice. This method is based around a sling with the ability to quickly adjust the length without much difficulty. To get in this position, the sling is looped around the body, coming over the firing-side shoulder and under the support-side arm.

"Patrol carry"

When the rifle is rested upon a barricade/obstacle, the sling is tightened so when the shoulders are squared to the rifle the increased tension locks the rifle in place and reduces the wobble area. Changing the position of the support arm can also increase, or decrease, the sling tension. This method can also function in a similar manner as the regular slung unsupported positions, just without the cuff.

Utilizing the patrol carry to tighten up a shooting position.

Benefits to this style of employment are mobility, ease of use, and ease of setup. Positions can be changed quickly with the sling around the body without any sacrifice of speed. The rifle remains slung on the body to be used in the same manner in almost any position, which can save time changing positions. No additional gear besides the adjustable sling is required for this technique to work. If thick jackets with hoods, backpacks, or other gear are being worn, using the sling in this manner may cause hang ups on these items. Nothing you can't work around, but be sure to practice this method with different seasonal/situational clothing arrangements.

The other method mentioned was clipping the rear portion of the sling into the belt. Clipping into the belt is preferable to the belt loop due to the high chance of the stitching on the belt loop coming undone. Clipping the sling into the belt increases tension in the position which helps control muzzle rise through recoil, as well as reducing the wobble area.

Carabiner clipped into the belt.

To make this happen, all the shooter needs to do after clipping into the belt is relax the hips back. Do not confuse this with actively pulling back with the hips, relaxing them down/back provides plenty of tension. Different positions will obviously dictate the position of the hips and how much rearward force they can apply. Experiment with how much tension is comfortable and effective for each position.

A relaxed kneeling position with the sling providing tension to tighten the wobble area.

The shooter still remains very mobile, much like the previous method, and rifle handling is not impacted negatively in most situations. A carabiner (or some sort of gear clip) is required to make this method work, as well as an area in the rear of the sling to clip into, making this method slightly more difficult to set up initially. Getting out of the sling is fast and easy, but the rear of the sling will still need to be reattached to the rifle to keep the sling out of the way. If the sling has enough quick adjustment, the clip-in technique can be used to aid any position ranging from prone on rooftops to standing positions.

A clipped-in sling providing additional stability to a standing position.

Different body types and gear setups will determine which method will have the most success for the individual. If an adjustable sling is not in your current inventory, reach out to friends and local shooters to try different slings out to find the one that fits your needs best. The Rifle's Only carbine sling has a bungee portion that reportedly aids stabilization in the patrol carry method. Short Action Precision's sling specializes in a quick-release cuff that is useful to get quickly out of a standard slung position. And TAB's Pinnacle Rifle Sling has a built-in carabiner loop, as well as reinforced sections for helping support the rifle in the front and rear. Each one of these slings has quick-adjust capabilities while bringing something different to the table to fit your individual needs.

A reinforced portion of the TAB Pinnacle Rifle Sling providing support for a low prone position.

Real World and Competition Position Comparisons

Competition can be a great aid to anyone looking to improve their shooting ability. The competition circuit is not the end all, be all, but it certainly drives home proficiency with a rifle and a familiarity with one's gear. This proficiency eventually rises to a level where building the position and steadying the rifle for the shot becomes a subconscious action, freeing up immediate mental focus for other highly variable factors such as wind and target location. When approaching a competition and seeing the different barricades and obstacles there, remember how the body is positioned for each varying height and how your body is forced to conform to certain obstacles. While nature doesn't always have pretty barricades and rooftops, you are still put in similar positions that are found in competition. The support changes, but the position remains more or less the same.

The big takeaway is position prediction, rifle proficiency, and keeping a wide field of view. Imagine yourself hunting and a big buck is spotted from across a field. There is no support in the immediate area, and the ground is covered in tall grass, eliminating any hope for a prone shot. But if you open up your field of view and notice that perhaps 10-15 yards to the left there is a fence or large rock outcropping that would aid in building a solid position. However, there are opportunity costs to everything. If you know from previous match and practice experience that you can throw a pack down and are solid shooting seated from the top of that pack, it might be the better choice and will save a good amount of time and should thus forego the position on the fence.

On the other hand, if you know that you are not stable from any of the options in the immediate area, it would be best to make a quick movement to the fence/rock and build a position there. Already knowing how to build that position frees up your focus to concentrate on more important tasks, such as keeping your eyes downrange on the target so as not to lose it, as well as being able to take wind indicators into account. Being able to efficiently build and break solid positions results in the shooter engaging targets faster and with increased accuracy.

4 Bags and Backpacks

The use of rear bags has exploded in popularity in the past few years. Bags of all shapes and sizes are available to shooters these days that can be tailored to specific shooting styles. One of the more important developments of these bags is the use of very light microbeads that make maneuvering the bag a breeze. These microbeads are impervious to the effects of moisture and can easily be squished to fit where the rifle needs support. The size of bags have also grown to support the rifle better in positions with large gaps.

Behold, my bags!

Using these large bags as front supports can be desirable when firing from uneven surfaces with lots of edges, such as boulders and jagged rocks. A large bag allows the rifle to be rested anywhere on the obstacle's surface, rather than nitpick and fine tune the bipod legs to get the rifle level. This also helps to reduce hop and felt recoil during firing. When looking at a hard surface, it is typically best practice to not rest hard surfaces on other hard surfaces. If a soft medium can be employed, it will typically benefit the position.

The advantages of running these bags are that they are extremely lightweight for their size and can be quickly placed in and out of position. They are easy to keep out of the way when not needed and aren't cumbersome to maneuver with, due to the lightweight materials. Competition shooters will often have a wide range of bags to choose from for different scenarios. This is all personal preference, just like with anything else, but I find that I can accomplish everything I need with 1 - 2 bags maximum.

I often see shooters bring a caravan of XL bags to matches, only to watch them not utilize any of them effectively. Buying more gear and bags does not equate to immediately becoming a better shooter. This isn't a gear race. Simply knowing how to employ the gear that you have now is infinitely more beneficial than buying the newest piece of cool gear that everyone on the internet touts as a "game changer."

I think we all know this, but reality can often become distorted in the excitement of a new purchase. I've seen countless shooters mount pillows on their arms to take standing shots from a barricade where the bags serve no purpose there. Another observed situation is in kneeling positions where the bag is pushed to the side of the arm, so it doesn't even contact the support knee, or the wrong knee is up so the arm and bag have nothing to be supported by. If your arm can already contact your knee without the aid of a pillow, use that pillow to try and make contact with the buttstock of the rifle. Supporting the buttstock will aid the position while hanging a pillow off the arm does nothing.

Practice with the gear and bags that will be used when it's time to perform until suitable proficiency has been achieved. Know how to use each piece of gear best in different positions. If a lower kneeling position is being used where the elbow bag isn't needed, try to place the bag in between the buttstock and the leg to provide another point of contact and support. Always search for additional points of contact. Bags are great at maximizing surface area, but getting carried away with the bags can be detrimental when the shooter becomes dependent upon them.

Backpacks

My go-to technique for filling large voids in my position is utilizing the pack that I already have with me. I use a cross sling technique that a good buddy of mine and I have developed and played with over the past few years. The cross sling allows the pack to be quickly slung out of the way when not in use and quickly employed to provide additional support for the firing elbow, or buttstock of the rifle. While the pack can be a little more cumbersome than simply stacking lightweight bags on top of one another, I prefer the utility of using the gear that I will almost always have with me.

To cross sling correctly, start with a pack slung on the strong-side shoulder.

Bring strong-side strap over the head and that's it, you are set!

The backpack has also aided me in the stabilization of nearly every position, so it is versatile while remaining practical. The backpack contains many items that are of use to me such as warming and waterproofing layers that provide good stuffing, small tools for the rifle and optic, cleaning rags and supplies, etc. Obviously, the issue of weight can quickly come into play so I always keep my pack as light as possible, so the weight doesn't become a burden.

The backpack has proven its worth to me in a variety of positions. In high-prone positions where rear bags won't come close to supporting the rifle, the backpack slung in front gives a place for my chest, as well as the rifle, to rest which results in a very stable position. The pack can also fill more gaps than just a single large bag (depending on backpack used), especially in high-kneeling positions. Being able to support the firing-side elbow can make all the difference in those stretched out, high-kneeling situations. The pack also provides a very stable platform to support seated positions by simply resting the entire rifle on the bag, seen in the earlier section on sitting.

A pack fills the large gap to support the elbow and buttstock in a high-kneeling position.

5 Rooftops, Slopes, & Tank Traps

Roof tops are a common occurrence at any match put on these days, as well as a potential obstacle surrounding us in our day-to-day lives. For the standard rooftop position, it will be sloping down towards you and the firing position will be from over the top. There are different ways to approach this position and depending on what gear is available to you; everyone has their favorite. For example, some shooters like placing a small bag up front between the stock and rooftop. The bag provides more surface area than resting the stock on the corner of the rooftop and can also help deaden some of the bounce from recoil.

One approach to rooftop positions is tucking both legs up "froggy style" with the shoulders square to the rifle and have a backpack or bag in between the legs to fill that void between the rifle and the rooftop/top of the leg. If the bipod is still attached, use it to hook over the lip of the rooftop. This can aid in keeping the reticle on target more effectively by letting the bipod/rifle absorb most of the recoil coming back towards you.

Shooting a rooftop stage in competition "froggy style."

Froggy style on the rooftop.

Another option is to lay "side saddle" on the roof. Here, you simply lay on your support side and fill the void between the buttstock and the rooftop as best you can. This position can be better suited for those with knee injuries. Side saddle may also be the better option if you have an elevated heart rate from physical activity. The large arteries in your legs aren't pinched as much as they are with having both legs tucked up. Laying the legs down the slope of the rooftop can also be less strenuous to maintain for extended periods if the rooftop isn't too steep.

The "side saddle" rooftop position.

If the rooftop slant continues down the opposite side from you, a bipod can be deployed and rested on the forward slant. This is often the quickest solution and provides a very steady support.

What shouldn't happen on a rooftop is deploying the bipod legs and resting them on the slope that is facing us before reaching the apex. This creates a larger gap between the buttstock and any support, resulting in the position being more difficult to stabilize. Remember to get as low as is comfortable, both you and the rifle. If multiple shots are being taken from this position, recoil forces the rifle further down on the slope which means the barrel inches closer to resting on the rooftop. The barrel should not be resting on anything, doing so will cause the shot to go higher than intended and miss the target. The next time a rooftop position is encountered, keep these solutions in mind and discover which one works best for you given the circumstances.

This bipod placement on the roof increases the risk for barrel contact after multiple shots, or during target transitions.

Reverse Rooftops/Slopes

Reverse rooftops and slopes often throw shooters far outside their comfort zone when first encountered. If the slope is shallow enough, the only thing that needs to be done is employ taller bipods. Another option would be to place the shorter bipod legs on top of a pack, or another medium, to sufficiently raise the front of the rifle to engage the targets. As for the length of deployed bipod legs, overestimating the amount of height needed is always better than underestimating. Adjusting most bipod legs to bring the rifle down is typically easier and faster than trying to adjust the rifle up. Shifting the bipod attachment point on the handguard, or rest that is being used, closer to the rear also provides some additional vertical adjustment.

In situations where the downward slope is too steep to lay prone, extra-long bipods are extremely valuable. Shooting sticks also come in handy and can provide a decent position. Tripods can also be utilized, but often take far too long to set up and are usually done so haphazardly.

Utilizing long bipods to overcome the reverse slope.

If long bipods are not available, or the slope is too steep, leaning back and to the side against the slope while resting the rifle on a backpack placed between the legs is a solid alternative. Leaning on the side and staying lower to the surface aids in our relaxation of the position. If only the lower back is laid upon, the abdominal muscles are forced to maintain the torso in an upright position.

Below, a bipod and pack are being used effectively, but the abs are doing excessive work to keep the torso upright.

The rifle is slightly out of the shoulder pocket with the pack secured by the legs. Abs are much more relaxed since the torso is supported by the slope.

Below is another example of a shooter using a pack and a standard bipod to obtain the required amount of elevation.

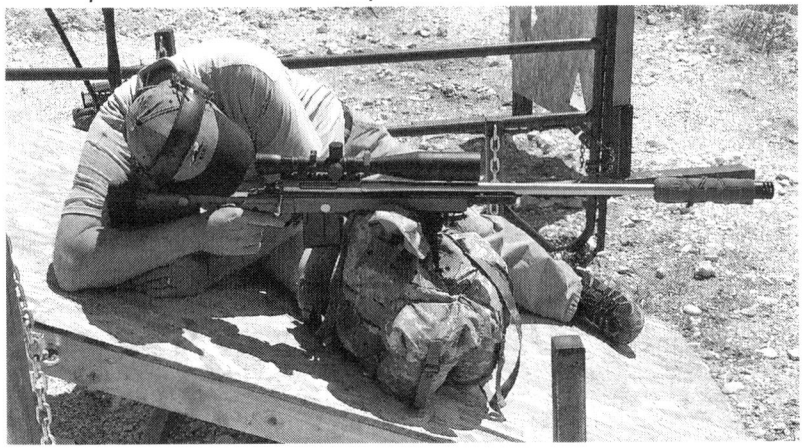

Side Slopes

Side-sloping rooftops can be easily tackled by adjusting one bipod leg fully up and the other leg all the way down (swiveling bipods are necessary for this!!), or even folding one leg up while extending the other one down to even out the rifle if the angle is steep enough. Depending on the side of the slope, it may also force you to either shoot from the support side or lay your whole body down head first on the slope perpendicular to the rifle. The latter option is less desirable and one I wouldn't recommend for *most* situations. The position takes longer to get in and out of and, depending on the severity of the slope angle, the shooter is constantly fighting gravity hanging head first while attempting to build a position and locate targets. It's more advantageous to get comfortable shooting from both sides.

A large bag, or backpack, can be used as rear support and the position can be made very stable. If firing from the support side, you'll find that it is difficult for the support hand to get a good trigger pull due to the incline on that side. Using the dominant hand to pull the trigger is much easier. This maintains grip familiarity with the trigger pull and reduces the overall strain of the position.

Notice I'm using my support shoulder while pulling the trigger with my strong-side hand.

When firing from a smaller side-sloping support (beams, railroad ties, etc.), a similar technique of shortening one bipod leg and lengthening the other can be used. Depending on the width of the beam supporting the rifle, recoil may force the rifle off the beam after the shot. To combat this, reaching the support hand forward and bracing the bipod leg against the barrier will help to maintain constant contact.

Adjustable bipod legs providing level support while the support hand maintains the position.

Utilizing the adjustable bipod legs on the opposite side of the slope.

Resting the handguard on the slant can also be a good choice. Supporting the stock from sliding down with the support hand, like in the other positions, is easy to do and you can take advantage of additional surface areas. If the bipod is still attached, it can also take some of the recoil force if hooked on the far side of the slant. This makes the barricade and rifle do the work to stopping recoil, rather than your shoulder. This is a case-by-case scenario since sometimes harder surfaces (such as a metal railing) can bounce the rifle off target through recoil. A bag can help to eliminate this problem if you choose to employ it.

Support hand providing support and maintaining rifle's position.

Support hand reaching under to maintain rifle's position.

Larger bags may also be used to overcome the problem of slanted surfaces. The bag's increased surface area makes supporting the rifle easy. The bag also greatly reduces the chance of the rifle falling from the position due to recoil.

The rifle is supported by a larger bag to help disperse recoil energy and maintain position.

Tank Traps

The tank trap can be intimidating to a new shooter with its sharp angles and protruding beams. Instead, it should be welcomed since the tank trap typically provides a solid low kneeling, or sometimes sitting position by resting the rifle in the crossing point of the structure. A rear bag can be placed in the crossing point to overcome the sharp angles of the beams and maximize the total surface area the rifle comes in contact with. The bag also can help with applying a downward force on the stock, or optic, to mash the rifle into a rock-solid position and better control recoil forces. Rear support can be utilized by other bags or backpacks, as well as the knees.

A bag being used to overcome the angles of the tank trap.

If a front bag is not an option, or you prefer not to use one, then deployed bipod legs can often find a good place to wedge on top of a beam. Tank traps present unpredictable angles so a stable position can often be built just by wedging the rifle stock in the corners. While this is often steady, the sacrifice made is increased difficulty making lateral adjustments if there are multiple targets to engage across the horizontal plane.

Bipods are wedged on top of an angled beam to provide support.

Another example of wedging the bipod where the posts meet, as well as using the backpack and bag for rear support.

Firing from the tips of the tank trap can also be tricky. I have had success with resting the bipod legs over the top and wedging them against the sides, similar to previous examples. Using a small bag on top of the point can also help by greatly increasing the surface area available for the stock to rest on. This largely depends on the density of the bag being used. If the bag isn't very dense, then the bag's contents will fall around the point, and you're still left resting the rifle directly on the point. Resting the stock itself directly on the point is the least favorable option since we have minimal surface area to take advantage of and are constantly having to fight to keep the rifle upright. If the angle of the beams lines up just right with the rifle while resting on the tips, you may be able to support a portion of the buttstock and gain more stability.

Bipod wedges on the top of a tank trap. Support hand will maintain the rifle's position through recoil.

Using a bag to increase surface area on the beam's point.

Firing position from only the tops of the beams. The rifle is supported by using a bag in the rear and wedging the bipods in the front.

Where tank traps put people out of their comfort zones is the protruding beams that often get in the way of where their head and limbs might otherwise rest. This in no way should have a large adverse effect on the stability of the shot, but it may require repositioning of the arms and legs. Some tank trap configurations will force you to wrap an arm or a leg around one of the posts to get into the best position possible. Tank traps are different every time, so come at them with a few ideas in mind and don't let a beam resting next to your head distract from the shot at hand. For the shooters out there that have no interest in competition, fallen trees, and thick branches can present similar problems that are found firing from tank traps.

6 Tripods, Bipods, & Shooting Sticks

The use of different length bipods and tripods is becoming more prevalent now than ever before. I've found that tripods, when used with the HOG/PIG saddle (from Shadow Tech LLC), can be one of the most versatile tools that a shooter owns. The saddle provides excellent support for the rifle, as well as binoculars, rangefinders, and anything else that the shooter can think of. A good technique, taught by USMC Scout Snipers and others, is the practice of clipping the rear of the sling into the belt as mentioned earlier. The sling provides excellent recoil management and firms up the position to the extent that standing shots from the tripod are relatively steady.

Sling tension providing additional stability with the tripod.

One of the detriments to the tripod is the amount of time spent setting it up. This can be mitigated by incorporating tripod practice into your regular dry-fire routine and out on the range. Making marks on the tripod legs that indicate standing, kneeling, or sitting positions can help take the guesswork out of setting it to the correct height for whatever position you need. Knowing that extending out one section of the legs gets you into "XYZ" position is valuable, time-saving knowledge that not many people take into account, or even care to learn. It is the same as position prediction for shooting from any other form of support.

Tripods that have adjustable center columns lend themselves to quicker fine-tuning adjustments once a position is built. Adjusting the center column's tension is much faster than breaking position to adjust multiple legs. However, the further up a column is adjusted, the less stable the position becomes. Keeping the center of gravity as low on the tripod as possible will provide the most stable position, as outlined in principle number 2, "get low". If the center column protrudes too far down and gets in the way of bushes, rocks, and other obstacles, remove a portion of the column. The whole column doesn't necessarily need to be removed (although that can be an option), but only enough to keep it out of the way while maintaining some adjustability.

A technique that I've used to great success is employing the tripod as a rear support in situations where there is already a solid front support. In the past, I had dabbled in placing a small bag on top of my PIG saddle to provide quick minor adjustments for the buttstock, but it was less than ideal. Any lateral adjustment was time-consuming and frustrating trying to get lined up on targets. I've since started using the tripod leg as a rear support by clamping the buttstock against the leg with the support hand, rather than supporting the buttstock with the center column.

Observe my left hand clamping the stock to the tripod leg.

This technique is preferable to the previous one for a few reasons. First, I was much more steady, and the tripod was less susceptible to tipping over since the weight was not being supported on the very top of the tripod. Secondly, this method is quicker and more flexible in regards to the lateral and vertical adjustment of the rifle. Since the tripod leg is splayed out at an angle, moving the tripod left and right gives you all the lateral and vertical adjustment needed in one quick motion. This makes transitioning between targets much quicker and more effective than any other method I've tried with the tripod as a rear rest.

However, this technique is not without its drawbacks. Recoil management can suffer depending on the position, so running optics on a slightly lower than usual magnification is recommended to maintain some self-spotting ability. Another drawback is space considerations. The best way to use this technique is fully deploying the tripod legs. This opens up the total area of adjustment available and gives more room for the firing arm to wrap around to get into position.

This obviously takes up larger amounts of space around the shooter, which may not always be an option when working in confined or uncomfortable spaces. Uneven or rocky ground can also slow down and complicate the position. This technique is best suited for somewhat static positions where there isn't much movement around other obstacles such as doorways, large rocks, furniture, etc.

Bipods & Shooting Sticks

Longer bipods can provide quick adjustment to get the rifle over an obstacle while still providing a steady platform. Many hunters certainly know the benefits of using these bipods. They provide quick elevation adjustment and are lightweight. Little to no extra effort is needed during movement since they are attached directly to the rifle, so mobility remains high. This also frees up the hands to work on other tasks needed in movement or building a position. The length of the legs may hinder maneuvering though since longer legs have a tendency of reaching out and grabbing nearby things. Having picatinny rails with quick-detach bipod attachments are ideal for speedy swapping, or ditching of bipods if needed.

Shooting sticks can also be a great tool to provide a steady front or rear rest. The sticks are typically very lightweight and easy to pack around, which makes the decision to bring them along easier when hiking. However, they can take longer to set up and build a position with when compared to bipods, and adjusting between different heights can be troublesome at times (depends on the type of shooting stick). Managing recoil off of shooting sticks can also sometimes be less favorable than other options since you can't load into the position. Shooting sticks are a great tool for single shots that need to be taken in the field, but if there are multiple positions and multiple shots needing to be fired within a time limit, investing in some longer bipods may be advantageous.

Shooting sticks used with a tripod result in a very steady position.

Using shooting sticks as a rear rest if a front rest is already available proves to be a very steady option. Depending on the type of shooting sticks used, elevation adjustments for the rear of the rifle can be made quickly by adjusting the legs wider/narrower, or positioning the legs further to the front or rear. Keep your mind open to different ways that the versatile shooting sticks can help steady different positions.

7 Support-Side Shooting

Shooting from the support side seems to be the bane of every shooter. This is also the reason that nobody seems to practice it very much because it isn't as fun and feels weird. These are exactly the reasons why support-side shooting should be practiced! The hardest thing to overcome is usually the use of the non-dominate eye. Some people cannot close their dominant eye, and this makes focusing the other eye through the optic extremely difficult. If you can close the dominant eyelid, then the problem isn't quite as bad, but it is still a challenge since the other eye isn't used to doing this much work. Luckily, our eyes are extremely adaptable, and with consistent practice using the other eye it shouldn't feel nearly as foreign. Dedicate five minutes at the end of each shooting session to getting comfortable switching the rifle from the dominant side to support side and getting the other eye to focus. Dry fire practice at home will, again, be the most beneficial way to solve this problem.

A technique that is often brought up in conversation is the use of tape over the shooting glasses so the dominate eye can't try to override the support eye. This works well in static positions with few targets and a relaxed environment. However, once there are multiple targets and different positions, you can see how this could be a detriment. Best practice would be to put the time in behind the gun and get your body and eye used to the position.

A good approach would be to start out prone, then move to sitting, kneeling, standing, etc. Get as comfortable as possible switching sides in that position before moving up to the next highest position.

Try to mimic your strong-side position on support side as much as possible. The shooter can easily get caught up in dealing with the wobble they see through the optic and ignore how their body is positioned. Practice pulling the trigger with both the support hand and strong hand.

Another thing that is often overlooked when shooting support side is bolt manipulation and magazine changes. Most positions will still allow the dominant hand to manipulate the bolt, which will be the most efficient way since that hand is still on the bolt side of the rifle. The angle changes slightly and will feel a little different, so becoming proficient at decent bolt manipulation while shooting from the support side will help with efficiency. Being able to manipulate the bolt from both shoulders only helps and never hurts while providing better flexibility in selecting firing positions.

The same goes for magazine changes; these should be done with both hands. I constantly find myself using both hands to change magazines from the various positions I may be in. While we aren't trying to be whiz-bang 3-gun speed reloaders, an efficient magazine change can shave quite a few seconds off the time taken to re-engage after dropping the empty magazine.

Everyone has different techniques for indexing their magazine and with so many types of bottom metal on the market, there is no single best way. For me, I find it easiest with my rifles to index the front or rear portion of the magazine in the well first, and then rock the rest of the magazine into the rifle rather than just trying to shove the entire thing in at once. Again, this is with my bottom metal and rifle, so this won't always be the best way for everyone's unique setup.

Slightly exaggerated rear index of the magazine.

Indexing the front of the magazine in the bottom metal.

8 Bolt Manipulation

Bolt manipulation, when done properly and consistently, will always benefit you in whatever situation you find yourself in whether it is a competition, hunting, or just casually shooting long range. To stay ahead of wind changes and to make quick follow-up shots, you need to be able to work the bolt quickly and efficiently. The first area of concentration is maintaining a cheek weld while working the bolt. This is probably the most common mistake that I observe in classes/matches/etc., and will save the shooter a surprising amount of time between shots.

If you do this, I suggest recording yourself and counting the seconds taken after the shot for the head to come off the stock and reacquire the sight picture. I have observed the average shooter takes around 2-4 seconds longer to reacquire their sight picture and fire again when their head is lifted between shots. Initially, this doesn't seem like much time, but combined over multiple shots, this can lead to be a significant waste of time. Doesn't sound like much initially, but add that up over the course of multiple shots and you can see how much wasted time that can amount to. This does not lend itself to consistency, nor a good economy of motion, since you are obtaining a new sight picture for every single shot, rather than maintaining the cheek weld and keeping the same sight picture for the entire string of fire.

The second area of concentration is maintaining a good economy of motion throughout the whole process. There are a few different ways to grip the bolt with most being a variation of the full-fist and the knife-hand techniques. Both techniques have pros and cons. For example, the full-fist has very positive control of the bolt handle with little chance of the hand slipping off. This can be advantageous in very dirty environments where the action has become gritty and more difficult to work than usual, or in the cold where the extremities don't want to move quite as well as they did before. However, this technique requires slightly more movement than is necessary to work the bolt since the entire hand comes off the stock and must reach forward to the handle before any work is imparted upon the bolt.

Full-fist technique.

The knife-hand technique uses the thumb to help cantilever the forward stretched fingers to lift the bolt and begin bringing it to the rear. This technique provides very little to no wasted movement in lifting the bolt. However, depending on the outside conditions, exact technique used, and style of bolt handle, fingers slipping off the bolt can happen more often than with other techniques. This usually happens when the shooter is trying to work the bolt very quickly and then the proverbial wheels come off. Stutters in bolt manipulation are caused largely in part by not working the pattern enough to become instinctively proficient at different speeds, or just rushing it past their point of proficiency (something we all do).

Knife-hand technique.

I use somewhat of a hybrid technique. My thumb cantilevers on the stock in the same manner as the knife hand so the bolt handle is contacted immediately in the upward motion. The way my fingers lay is where the process differs. While most of the bolt is enclosed in my hand, the bolt knob isn't sunk as deep into my palm as it is with the full-fist technique. As my hand begins lifting the bolt upwards, the knob is caught on the middle knuckle of my middle finger while the pointer finger wraps around the edge. This provides a good amount of contact area to prevent slippage when running the bolt quickly.

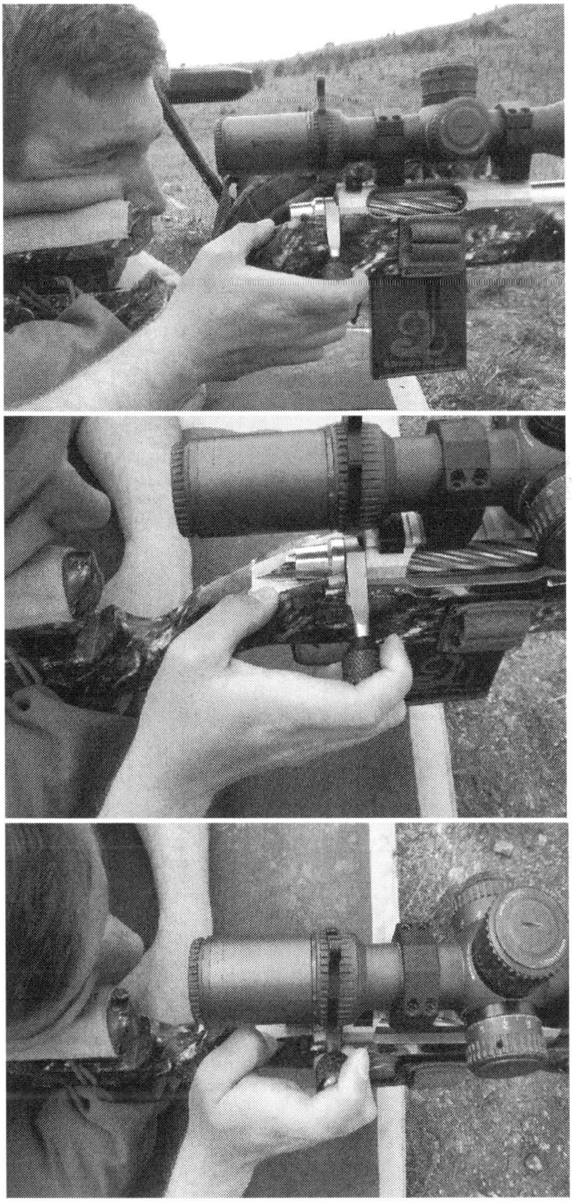

Proper dry fire is the key to ensuring a smooth and consistent bolt cycle. There is no such thing as too much slow-fire practice, especially when it comes to this. For things to work at high speed, they need to function flawlessly, and consistent patterns should be practiced before every dry fire and live-fire session. While practicing the bolt stroke, try not to think of the movements as up-back-forward-down (4 straight line motions). Think in your head while you're manipulating the bolt that it is an arc to the rear, and an arc to the front. Just changing the way I thought about the bolt cycle process helped me to smooth out and make it not so clunky.

One of the other areas where I notice myself, and other shooters, momentarily getting hung up is when the bolt is fully to the rear of the cycle. Excluding any issues with the magazine feeding correctly, the bolt can sometimes bind for a moment, or not move as smoothly when there is too much upward pressure is being applied. This happens since the bolt head is the only portion making contact with the receiver and thus, more "wiggle" can be induced. The position of the upward lifted bolt handle also easily lends itself to applying an excess amount of upward force which can halt, or stutter-step the cycle of the bolt.

A small amount of grease can be applied on the top rear portion of the action to increase the lubricity, but the most consistent way to avoid this problem is imparting a slight downward force on the bolt. If I start having trouble with this, I literally start saying "down" to myself in my head as I'm cycling to bolt forward to remember to provide some downward pressure that keeps the bolt in motion and free from binding. The pressure is very slight though; we aren't trying to push the bolt through the bottom of the action! Visualizing a smooth bolt cycle beforehand also greatly benefits the consistency of the manipulation.

Once proficiency has been obtained with the bolt manipulation, it is important to practice running the bolt from a variety of different positions. You will quickly realize that some positions will require slight modifications to the grip on the bolt and especially the speed that it is done. Running the bolt extremely fast is not always the best option. This is why proficiency at all speeds must be achieved, and consistency is stressed. Through practice, you will discover which bolt speeds are appropriate for different situations with your body and rifle set up. For myself, I run the bolt very quickly when I am in a solid position where I can spot my shots easily, and my firing arm has good stability (typically prone, or lower positions). I tend to slow down in less stable positions, or when I'm focusing on accuracy.

Be careful not to feel rushed when trying to run the bolt quickly, since these rushed actions often don't stop when the bolt closes and follows to the trigger pull; the one area that should not be rushed! If you can change gears from rapidly running the bolt back down to focusing on that trigger, there should be no detrimental effects on your shooting. If you find yourself continually making bad trigger presses after rapid bolt manipulation, you need to slow down on the bolt and focus on what you are doing. Extreme speed isn't necessary, making the bolt cycle smooth and consistent is much more important!

9 Shot Procedures

Every shooter should build a set of shot procedures, or a list of things that are done in preparation for the shot, the shot itself, and after shooting is completed. These lists can vary for different people, but should follow the same general outline. Mistakes will always be made in whatever we do, but steps should be taken to reduce or eliminate the chance of the same recurring mistakes.

The most efficient way of doing so is to write things down and make lists. It's not flashy or fun, and gets a little mundane at times, but recording areas where you have found difficulty will help you to recall it much easier than trying to remember what happened two weeks ago. I hear shooters say all the time that they'll take their notes at the end of a day of shooting. While most issues can be recalled, the specifics of the position and shot often cannot. Take the extra 20 seconds to jot down exactly what gave you difficulty after a bad shot.

As these mistakes accumulate, a specific and systematic approach can be taken to remedy them. Easy mistakes such as having the wrong dope dialed for the first shot, not loading enough rounds in a magazine (I double count all of my rounds), or firing a shot at the wrong target all have negative consequences. I'll list my personal shot procedures that I've developed for myself below, and explain why I have them and in the order that they are in.

1. **Identify Target** – The first step should be obvious, but we have to find and range our target before it can be engaged. Be sure

to keep an open field of view when scanning and ranging to provide good reference points. Reference points should guide your eyes to the target location with little difficulty. I find it easiest to go from big to small in terms of reference points. When I start "big," I'll try to find a large object or terrain feature that I can see with the naked eye that points me in the direction of the target. Things such as peaks, draws, groves of trees, etc. While ranging through the optic, take note of smaller features observed with magnification that guide you to the target. Things such as rock features, unique trees/bushes, and trails. Doing these things consistently will save large amounts of time in acquiring targets.

2. **Dial Dope on Turrets** — This is done before I even start to build a position. Rough wind calls have been made by this point, and I'm dialing in my elevation. I want to do this before everything else because for me, once I start building the position and scanning downrange it becomes easy to get caught up in looking through the glass for the target, or steadying the rifle. Your focus is almost entirely on what is happening through that scope, especially if things are constantly changing downrange. Dialing the turrets after a position has been built can also be a waste of time and may force you to rebuild part of the position by bringing your hand in and out. If holdovers are in play, this step just becomes a mental confirmation of the elevation that is about to be used.

3. **Set the Rifle First** – I prefer setting the rifle down or getting the front of the rifle supported before I begin building any position. Supporting the rifle first greatly reduces the amount of work/conscious thought that is required to keep the rifle pointed in a safe direction (and in the target's direction), and frees up an extra hand to aid in building a solid position, rather than holding the rifle up.

4.   **Target, Rifle, Body** – Going hand-in-hand with the previous step, getting the rifle first oriented towards the target will eliminate the error of getting a comfy position built, only to discover that you're not pointed in the right direction. I know I have done this, and I watch someone do the same at nearly every match I attend, so I believe it's an important concept to master.

The best way to avoid getting sucked into focusing solely on your position is keeping your head up. As soon as my rifle is set, my head is up and looking for the target area again. Building the position should begin as you orient the body towards the target. This also aids in attaining a good natural point of aim from whatever position you're in. Having a good natural point of aim is not always possible in some of these positions, but you should seek it out whenever you can.

5.   **Power Down Optic & Scan** – Reducing the magnification of the optic opens up a wider field of view observed downrange. This obviously makes acquiring targets much faster, especially when there are multiple targets to engage. While scanning, I'm also looking for those identifying features that I noted previously to help guide me to the target.

6.   **Power Up, Final Preparation** – Once the target has been acquired, increase magnification to a comfortable level that will still allow the impact, or miss, to be spotted through recoil. Take a second to realize any wind changes at your position and if there is any vegetation downrange to indicate dramatic changes in the wind between you and the target. Any final, minor tweaks to the position are made, one last exhale and properly timing the trigger pull will round out the shot procedures.

This was just one list of procedures that can, and should, be made (depending on skill level) until it becomes part of the subconscious. I don't have to think consciously of each item on the list since I have been able to practice them long enough where these processes automatically happen.

Creating a shooter's checklist for packing gear is also a valuable practice. It's easy, doesn't take much time, and is a process that can only help improve the shooting experience. Going through the list helps reduce the chances of accidentally forgetting something back at the house as well. As more positions and situations are encountered, a list also aids in determining what additional gear will be beneficial, as well as seeing what gear is unneeded and can be removed from the current list.

10 Importance of Dry-Fire Practice

I am a huge proponent of dry-fire practice. Dry fire is absolutely necessary to becoming a better shooter, and aids in truly understanding how all of the gear that is available to you can be used together. I say that matches are won at home because that is where the bulk of the rifle practice can, and should, be done.

Improvements should not entirely be made on the range. If that's the only place you practice you either have an excess of time, money, or more than likely both. Which isn't a bad thing, but there are more cost-effective ways to go about these things. The material costs for dry-fire practice are essentially zero; you already have your rifle and can use any household item around to help serve as a barricade or obstacle. No ammunition is consumed and thus no barrel wear occurs, saving your barrel life for when it needs to be used on a hunt, a match, etc.

Dry-fire practice also has minimal time requirements since no travel is required to and from a range (unless you're one of those bastards who have a range in their backyard). If you have children around the house, you most likely have an excess of toys, playsets, or play cars around the house as well. Put them to good use! Build positions from scooters, car seats, large push cars, chairs, tables, swing sets, anything!

I particularly enjoy using odd items around the house that are never found in matches because the items present a completely new problem that hasn't been faced before; this forces creativity to build the most solid position as possible. Things with wheels, such as a skateboard, can turn a typically stable barricade into a frustrating one. Learn to work through the problems presented and take note of what works best in any given position that can be used later.

The use of scaled targets can make dry-fire sessions extremely productive. Knowing the approximate size of the target gives a consistent reference point to evaluate how steady a position is without having to worry about mirage, wind, and other factors that can affect the shot and position. Referencing your wobble area against the observed target size gives a good indicator as to how successful the shot from that position could have been during live fire. Known target sizes also help determine whether or not the body position/gear used is more, or less effective than other alternatives.

Print out your own targets that are scaled appropriately for the distance they will be used. Or, if you already have certain items you dry fire at such as a bolt head or a speck on the wall, take a minute to measure the size of the item in your reticle. Be sure to write the size down, so you don't have to keep measuring the item in the reticle because you forgot. This should help to give you the reference needed for accurately gauging positional stability.

Position prediction is a useful concept that will save huge amounts of time in building that initial position once you encounter an obstacle. Position prediction is exactly what it sounds like; predicting what position you will place your body, gear, and rifle in for the obstacle encountered. Building a position takes the largest amount of time for the shot, especially if the current position isn't the best and needs rebuilding. My position prediction is almost entirely improved upon with dry fire practice. When looking at an obstacle, keep the positional principles (*Support front of rifle, support elbow/rear of rifle, and get as low as is comfortable*) in mind and imagine how you would place yourself to build the best position possible.

Most importantly, consistent dry-fire practice builds proficiency in the ability to call one's shot. This is a huge concept that **must** be mastered. "Calling" the shot means a mental snapshot is taken of where the reticle was in relation to the target at the moment the trigger broke. This ability is gained only through practice with both live and dry fire. Accurately calling the shot requires that the shooter is completely honest about where that shot broke and leave pride/ego out of it.

None of us break perfectly centered shots every single time, and that is okay. Analyzing where the shot is called and where that shot actually went is a crucial point in shooting from alternative positions. If the fundamentals are not sound, calling the shot becomes frustrating since the bullet does not always go where the rifle was aimed due to the improper execution of the fundamentals.

Until the fundamentals have been at least somewhat ingrained, I would recommend holding off on extensive positional shooting. A strong base of dry fire builds confidence in positions and knowing that the bullet will go wherever the reticle is aimed.

Dry Fire Enablers

The obstacle we all face with dry fire are these highly magnified optics that most of us use. Most scopes do not focus down to 9 yards or less (unless you're shooting a Schmidt and Bender or

March Optics scope), which is a typical distance that can be found in most households. Don't worry, there are ways around this! The Indoor Optical Training Aid (IOTA) can be used to help create a parallax-free image in cramped spaces. Quality mirrors can also be arranged to reflect the image of your target, and thus increasing the optical range to adjust the parallax for your optic. This is extremely difficult to do correctly, since arranging the mirrors isn't easy and they must be of higher quality. The IOTA is the best option due to the image quality, ease of setup, flexibility, and the amount of space required for it to function (~11 feet).

I promise that if a consistent and structured dry fire regimen is implemented, you will see an improvement in your shooting! The crazier the obstacles that are found, the better. If the obstacle forces the mind to think creatively, that is what you want to be using!

An example of a standard positional dry-fire session might include:

-- Warm up prone, focusing on perfect trigger presses, breathing, and bolt manipulation   **10 presses**

-- Begin working up from the belly (high prone or seated position) on a 1 to 1.5 MOA dot   **10 presses**

-- Kneeling positions of varying heights at 1 to 2 MOA dots (building/breaking position each time)   **10-15 presses each**

-- Standing with front support at 2 MOA dots
    10 presses (take your time, pay attention to breathing cycle, build and break position)

-- Set up multiple aiming points across the wall at varying heights, begin timed evolutions that incorporate finding and engaging different targets.

-- 2 minutes to engage 5 targets with two presses each. Three to four positions are to be utilized.

-- Repeat and alter as desired, finish by focusing on breaking down positions that you have had difficulty with during the session or in the past.

11 Training Regimen

What is practiced in dry fire is later confirmed through live fire. While dry fire is an incredibly effective training tool, practicing without a purpose can delay, or inhibit obtaining the desired results. I recommend conducting dry and live-fire training with a structured approach. Pick no more than 3 major concepts, or positions, that need attention and stick to practicing those 2-3 things for at least two weeks (assuming dry fire is happening every day or every other day). Sticking to the 2-3 concepts for a period of time helps the mind to explore the present positions and hopefully find different methods of approach.

A good ratio for your training objectives is making the first or last (user preference) concept trained a familiar one. If at the beginning, it can be used as a nice way to warm up and ease into the day's shooting. A good example could be a 100-yard dot drill, Know Your Limitations (targets of diminishing size) target array or a sitting position. These positions are stable enough that the fundamentals can be focused on to break those shots perfectly.

The second could be a technique or position that was attempted with sub-par results on a previous outing or helping reinforce a known position/concept. Examples might include hold-over drills or a barricade position of varying heights. Revisiting a position can be used to evaluate if the position can be adjusted for additional stability, or if it should be thrown out entirely for a more stable position/approach. Compare and contrast against these different positions and approaches and record your findings.

The third concept worked during a training session is really where the mind should be let free to create and modify. This is where you try completely new positions that have been observed from previous experiences, or new obstacles that have not been encountered. This newer material will usually take the bulk of the practice session due to the lack of experience and curiosity in finding the best position.

Never attempt a new position or gear layout when the shot is on the line and counts! I have done this multiple times, and I have seen countless other shooters attempt to alter something minutes before they are up to shoot in a match. Last-minute changes rarely work out in our favor. I would rather stick with a position that I have already practiced and know where I am going to place my gear and body. Attempting a brand new concept/position takes away from concentrating on the wind, target location, and fundamentals because most of the attention is directed towards attempting to figure out this new, weird position.

This is simply a suggested guideline, individual timelines and skills will vary. However, if you're new to the sport and have trouble with these unfamiliar positions, the overall cap of 3 concepts per session should remain. Shooting is fun, and one can easily be lulled into firing half the rounds that were brought from the prone position at all the targets.

Round Counts & After Actions

To help eliminate wasted rounds, I recommend no more than 50-60 rounds be brought to the range. This helps make each round count more than they would if 100+ rounds were brought. More rounds fired downrange does not equate to a higher quality of training. I have often been lulled into staying in one position (barricade, prone, etc.), and discovered that I had already fired a large portion of my rounds in a single position, rather than sticking to my plan and firing more rounds from different positions. There are certain exceptions to this round limit such as dot drills, load development, plans with buddies, and so on. The round limitation is placed exclusively on the developmental or positional portion of the shooting session.

An agenda should also be drawn up prior going to the range. Writing the information down, knowing exactly what you are going to practice that day, and how many rounds will be committed to each course of fire helps immensely to staying on track. The agenda also helps you remember that one little thing you have wanted to practice! I forget things all the time and find that recording the plan helps me have a productive practice session by not leaving anything out.

Writing down the day's shooting activities before arriving to the range also helps you stick to that list. I have tried writing the list down on my phone with less than stellar results. I found myself forgetting to open my phone to read the agenda, or just not wanting to and easily pushing it aside. With a physical paper copy of the list, it is right in front of my face where I can't hide from it!

If you are not keeping notes or some kind of after-action report, then you are missing out on a huge source of raw data that will help build future practice sessions. Consistent and informative notes need to be taken as soon as possible following the shooting activity. Record what positions gave you the most trouble and what you need to work on. Don't record only the bad things, be sure to record the things that **did** work to keep in the toolbox of skills.

Positive reinforcement of doing something right is just as important as realizing something is wrong. Shooters are often very hard on themselves regarding their shooting performance and can often get swallowed up in frustration. Being frustrated with our lack of performance is natural, so don't bother trying to "shake it off and act like it didn't happen." It did happen. Just be able to quickly realize what went wrong, and begin formulating a plan on how to prevent that problem from happening again in the future.

Time Limits and Physical Stressors

Once an acceptable level of proficiency has been obtained, start introducing stressors. Increase the heart rate before the practice stage with some sort of physical activity, or your favorite caffeine-packed beverage of death. When you are out of breath, and your heart is pounding, positions that were once solid are often more difficult than before. Be sure to take the time for that extra breath and make the shots count.

I find it is often easy to get caught up in rushing through steps after I just ran 200 yards with my gear and rifle. Practicing this helps so there are no surprises when the time comes to perform in a match or on a hunt. You already know how your body is going to react and know what steps are needed to combat the effects. Everyone's body and fitness level are different, but when my heart is beating out of my chest, I try to take about 3 slow, deep breaths and continue exhaling slowly as I approach my position. I continue this controlled breathing cycle while I shoot, and this assists getting my heart rate under control while helping to avoid rushing shots.

Time limits should be imposed to add another factor of urgency. As soon as that timer goes off, we often lose our game plan and start rushing to "beat" the timer. This is less than ideal for our mental state. Rushing through and getting 5/10 hits under the time limit will never beat 6/10 hits and going over the time limit. Try to use as much of the time as possible, especially if there are multiple positions. Save time by efficiently building/breaking positions, and moving quickly between the positions. Use the saved time to focus on steadying the rifle and timing the shot perfectly.

Once you start reliably meeting the established time limits for a certain course of fire you have drawn up with a 70-80+ percent hit ratio, start reducing the time limit or reduce the target size. Change only one variable at a time. A good rule of thumb to start out with for timing positional shots is about 10 seconds per shot. This is assuming that there are position changes within the course of fire. Don't fall below a 50 percent hit ratio for your drills though. If you start consistently falling below this then either increase the target size or add additional time.

Targets and Ranges

Target sizes are also important. If you are a brand new shooter and are not at all familiar with shooting from obstacles, I would recommend using around 3 MOA targets to begin with. This is a fairly generous target size and will help to build your confidence in the beginning. Once you start achieving the above mentioned hit ratio, reduce the target size by one-half MOA. Work toward the 70-80 percent hit-ratio before reducing the target size again.

Most of my positional practice is done within 300 yards with the average target size being about 2 MOA. All of us have different ranges available to us, so do not feel disadvantaged if you only have access to 100-yard ranges. Practicing positional shooting at ranges of 300 yards and less really lets you focus on the raw positional aspect. Environmental factors don't affect your bullet like they do at longer ranges, so you won't have to worry about those while building and experimenting with different positions.

Practicing at 100 yards should typically involve some sort of paper target, which can be used as a great training aid. Shooting paper is more beneficial in a lot of ways than shooting steel at these closer distances. For one, steel gets pounded pretty hard at distances less than 200 or 300 yards.

Secondly, shooting at steel doesn't give you any feedback on misses. More importantly, steel doesn't give you feedback on how far you missed by and where exactly that shot went. Keeping your paper practice targets also creates a tangible history of your progress. You can see exactly how accurate you were on any given day, how far your misses were from the intended target, and track if you are consistently shooting smaller targets with less "fliers."

Take note that a 2-MOA target at 800 yards is more difficult than a 2-MOA target at 100 yards. In terms of relative size, they are the same, but the 800-yard shot requires much more attention to detail. The wind will be the largest contributor to missed shots at that range, and any inconsistent velocities in your load will be evident. Compound all these things with shooting from a barricade and it is easy to become overwhelmed, so don't get too discouraged. On calm days long-range targets will be more doable but if it is a hurricane-force day then don't be ashamed to increase the target size slightly, decrease the distance, or lower the hit percentage expectancy.

Weather Considerations

Don't be deterred by bad weather when you go out shooting, whether it's rain, high winds, snow, or heat. If you don't go out in these conditions, you won't find the holes in your training/gear that would otherwise be unknown. High winds not only affect the bullet's trajectory but also affect your position. The type of barricade will also play a large part in how wind affects the shot. Unless it is very sturdy and thick, the barricade will be moving in the wind as well. Positional shooting in high wind sucks, no way around it. However, if you consistently practice in strong winds, you will no doubt become more skilled and be better prepared than fair-weather shooters.

Pay attention to keep water off of the eyepiece in the snow and rain whenever possible. Water on the eyepiece distorts your view, and attempting to wipe it off with your hand usually does not help your situation. Also be conscious not to exhale as you bring your head down to the stock when it is cold or wet outside. I have done this a few times, and the eyepiece is instantly fogged at the worst time possible. Wait to exhale once a good sight picture has already been obtained.

Shooting in the rain will also usually result in pressure spikes due to moisture accumulating on the cartridges and in the bore. This can also change the point of impact of your rifle, especially at further distances. Record the effects while out shooting in these conditions so that you know what to expect when certain criteria are met, and can be more prepared when the shot counts.

Keep the ammunition and bore of the rifle dry as much as possible! Periodically run a dry patch through the bore if conditions are continuously wet. Placing a balloon over the muzzle can also help keep unwanted moisture out of the bore during transport.

Break apart the rifle at the earliest convenience after extended shooting sessions in the rain! Regular post-rain maintenance should include dry patching the bore, removing the barreled action from the stock, and thoroughly wiping down all surfaces. Wipe out the area that the action sits in the stock, whether it is a chassis system or a bedded stock. Rust waits for no man, and enough water exposure can eventually damage even the best bedding jobs. Scope rings should also be inspected to remove moisture in the screws (brake cleaner works well) and between the scope tube and ring surface if the weather was very severe.

Video Recording

The use of video to record your stages and practice sessions can help immensely to identify bad habits that would otherwise go unnoticed. We all have a vision in our head of what we look like and what we are doing; video bridges the gap between the vision of what we think is going on with what is actually happening. Habits such as removing the head after every cycle of the bolt, or constantly needing to re-adjust in certain positions will be quickly be exposed.

As shooters, we also need to ask ourselves periodically, "Is my gear performing the job that I need it to do?" Again, video helps bridge the gap to identify what pieces of gear are necessary and what is excessive, or detrimental to your performance. Reviewing past video recordings has certainly helped me identify more efficient ways to employ the gear that I use. Diagnosing problems with the rifle's function are also easily identified by video review. Video can sometimes be a pain to arrange, especially if you are in a hurry, but it is well worth the time to set up.

I constantly review video from recent and past shoots. I recently noticed that after manipulating the bolt, my thumb on my firing hand would reach over too far left on my stock when reacquiring my grip. That thumb would then drift back over to its regular spot before I would break each shot. I had no idea I was doing this! While it didn't affect accuracy since the thumb would end up in the same spot, it was wasted movement. I would not fire until that thumb was back in its spot.

To remedy this, I cut out a small dot of hook-side velcro and placed it in the area that my thumb rested naturally. Upon recent video review, I can say this has fixed the issue, and my thumb no longer wanders. When my thumb comes across that small velcro patch, it knows to stop right there and thus, I have eliminated a wasted movement that was present for every shot.

While this is an incredibly tiny detail, I try to make every movement as efficient as possible. Focus on the big things first, such as your movements into and out of positions, before focusing your attention on the smaller details.

Range Buddies

Bringing someone with you to the range is a great benefit, not only to provide video support for each other but also for increasing the stress level in conjunction with imposed time limits. We are naturally competitive beings. Even if you don't consider yourself to be very competitive, everyone wants to perform well with what they are doing in front of others. We often get nervous as a result of people watching and must try to overcome this. The best way to overcome this nervousness is to jump head first into these situations!

Having someone observe and even compete with you during your practice sessions can build a healthy drive for proficiency, and get you more accustomed to performing while under third-party scrutiny. Include the timer, and you're pretty close to replicating match conditions! If that isn't enough for you, make friendly bets and have the loser buy lunch. Things change when the shots are on the line and misses have consequences. A fellow shooter and friend should encourage you to do better and help think of different positions and stage ideas that you otherwise wouldn't have.

Another thing that can help track your improvement is setting up a stage/test at the end of your shooting session that tests the cumulative skills that were worked on that day. Your buddy can help design and setup the test, and swap out with you once you have completed it. Shoot that same test at the beginning of your following practice session (assuming that you have continued to practice the positions through dry fire) and compare how your skills have improved in that given area over the course of a month or two. Compare your progress to hold each other accountable!

12 Standards & Time Trials

Drawing up your own drills and practice schedule is difficult if you don't have many previous experiences to call upon. The targets and drills listed below can be used to further your basic proficiency with the precision rifle both from the prone and alternate positions. Feel free to edit them to fit your personal training needs and create your own once specific task deficiencies have been identified. These targets (dot drill and positional analysis target) can be found easily online, and through the "Downloads" section of the Sidewinder Industries web page (www.sidewinderindustries.com).

Sniper's Hide Dot Drill –

This is a good drill to build proficiency in quickly finding and executing the fundamentals on a small target. It can be used to help warm up at the beginning of the day, as all the shots are from the prone, but still requires concentration. The descending time limits and start position variations can make this quite challenging once you get to the final targets. If you are new to firing from the support side, this will be good to ease you into the position as well. Here are the instructions for the Sniper's Hide Dot Drill, going down row by row of dots.

1. Single dot at the top engaged from the prone supported with two rounds in 30 seconds. It should take much less.

2. First row of 5 dots, with a magazine of 3 rounds and a second magazine of two, the shooter from the prone, magazine inserted, will fire 1 round per dot, then reload and complete the row with the final 2 rounds. Time limit to start with is 30 seconds.

3. Second row of 5 dots, with a magazine of 5 rounds inserted, the bolt back, shooter in the prone, put 1 round in each dot from the support side in 30 seconds.

4. Third row of 5 dots, rifle grounded with a magazine of 5 rounds inserted and the bolt back. The shooter starting from the standing will drop into the prone and fire 1 round in the first dot in 15 seconds and reset the drill and stand up. From there the shooter will repeat this with a descending time limit. 12 seconds, 10 seconds, 8 seconds, and finally 6 seconds for each shot.

5. Last row in the dot drill, the shooter starts standing with the rifle in hand, magazine inserted with the bolt back. At the start, drop to the prone and fire one round on the first dot in 30 seconds. Reset and stand up with the rifle, repeating the drill with a descending time limit of 25 sec, 20 seconds, 15 seconds and finally 10 seconds.

Sniper's Hide Dot Drill (SCP modified)

Cold Bore +1 / 30 seconds

○

3 rounds, magazine change, 2 rounds / 30 seconds

○ ○ ○ ○ ○

5 rounds support side / 30 seconds

○ ○ ○ ○ ○

Start standing behind grounded rifle

15 seconds   12 seconds   10 seconds   8 seconds   6 seconds

○ ○ ○ ○ ○

Start with rifle in hand

30 seconds   25 seconds   20 seconds   15 seconds   10 seconds

○ ○ ○ ○ ○

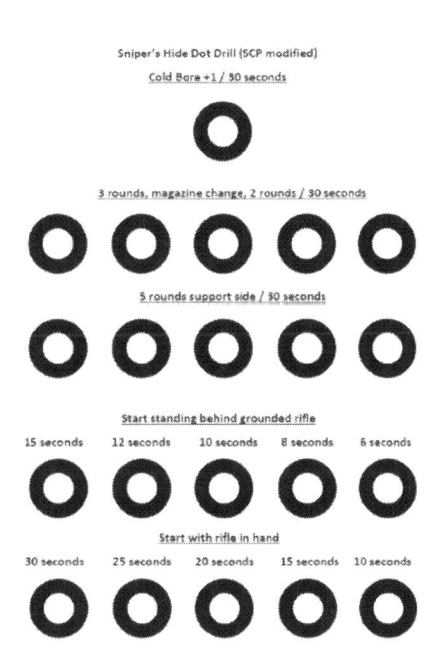

12 Second Position Building Drill –

Place a 2-MOA target at the distance of your choosing, typically a kneeling or sitting position, as these are the most commonly encountered positions. Start approximately 5 feet behind the barrier and try to make your shot in the 9.5 to 12-second range. This one is built to help those struggling with building positions in a timely manner. If the position is built quickly and efficiently, then you shouldn't feel rushed to break the shot. If you are feeling rushed, use video recordings to examine the way you build your position and the layout of the gear used.

As mentioned before, building positions take the largest amount of time before breaking a shot. If we can minimize the time required to get into the steadiest position possible, this will provide more time to spend on breaking the most perfect shot possible. If you are continuing to struggle to hit the 2 MOA target, increase the target size slightly and build your proficiency.

Building and Breaking Positions –

Use a target size and range of your choosing for this one. Start standing with your rifle and gear approximately 5 feet behind the barrier. Starting par time of 60 seconds. Adjust as needed.

    1st Shot – Prone
    2nd Shot – Kneeling position from barrier
    3rd Shot – Standing from barrier
    4th Shot – Sitting from barrier
    5th Shot – Back to prone, or a high prone from obstacle

I encourage one round per position. This will create more repetitions with the amount of rounds available while driving home the importance of making each round count. This drill also helps the shooter learn what gear will get in the way transitioning between different positions. Feel free to change the order of positions as well to fit your needs and training schedule.

Sidewinder Positional Analysis Target –

This simple 100-yard target can be used to analyze the shooter's accuracy for a given position, course of fire, time constraint, etc. The red dots along the top of the page can be used as up/down dot drills found in the previous dot drill, or speed dots where the final dot forces you to slow down and not get ahead of yourself. The large dots are ¾" and the small is ½". They can also be used to confirm zero for rifles at the beginning of the day.

If the dots are being used for speed drills, set a starting par time of 20 seconds beginning prone with bolt back. If they are being used in a similar fashion to the dot drill a decent beginning goal for par times would be 18, 15, 12, 10 and 8 seconds, starting with the rifle in hand, or on the ground, and going prone at the start signal.

The large target with rings is what you can use to record and analyze different positions, or gear setups. The outer black rings and center correspond with 1, 2, and 3 inch (MOA at 100 yards) target sizes. The white rings are the corresponding half inches (1.5 and 2.5). This allows you to quantify how accurate your shots are from any given position. The corresponding numbers on the side are there to record how many impacts were made within that diameter of ring.

The blank white 2" target can be used to evaluate what was just practiced on the ring target, but under a time limit or other physical stressor. Feel free to use and tweak to best fit your needs.

Examples of positional analysis target in use.

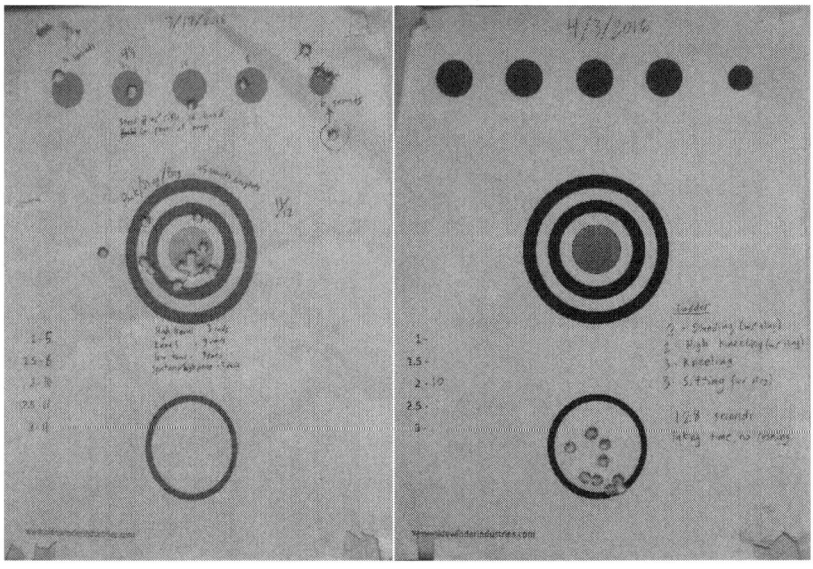

Run, Run, As Fast As You Can --

This drill can be used with the Sidewinder Positional Analysis Target. You will need 10 rounds, a ladder or barricade with 4 positions (standing, high kneeling, kneeling, sitting), and a 2-minute time limit. Do a brief 15-20 yard shuttle run (or other activity that raises the heart rate) and start the time once you get to your rifle. Fire 2 rounds from the standing position, 2 rounds from a high kneeling, 3 rounds from the lower kneeling and 3 final rounds from sitting.

This drill drives home the importance of managing your breathing and heart rate while changing positions safely and efficiently. Don't get flustered with the physical activity and let the run force you to lose concentration on the fundamentals of the shot. Aim for the 3" ringed circle/diamond to record your shots, or use the 3" ringed circle as a warm up run with no time limit to see how accurate you can be. Then use the smaller 2" circle/diamond below as the timed run.

Jim See's (of Elite Accuracy LLC) 40 Round Perfect PRS Practice --

Mr. See was kind enough to let me include this article of drills he has posted in various locations on the internet. I like the structure, and the drills follow what I have already gone over earlier relating to having specific tasks and sticking to round counts for efficient training. If you have a chance to learn from Jim at Elite Accuracy LLC, do so. He is one of the most consistent shooters in the country.

Barricade drills:

Approach barricade, build a solid position and fire 10 rounds at a 2-3 MOA target from different positions on a barricade. DO NOT time yourself. Once you can produce consistent hits start timing yourself at 2 minutes. Your goal is to build a solid position first, then engage your targets. Rushing through this program initially won't allow you to realize how stable you can be when you take your time. As you master the barricade put a clock on it. **10 rounds**

Prone accuracy training:

If you feel like you are anticipating each shot with an involuntary reaction, dry fire from prone. Process: aim on target using a stiff/hard rear bag, close your eyes for 3 seconds, dry fire, then open your eyes. Your crosshair should still be on a 1 MOA target.

Live-fire practice on 200 to 400-yard targets that are 1 MOA and smaller, I like .75 MOA. The shorter range takes some of the wind reading out of the equation but forces you to aim small and follow through for each shot. Concentrate on a smooth trigger pull, proper bag and cheek pressure will maintain your aim. This is where you work on your fundamentals of marksmanship. On my range, this drill is incorporated on a KYL rack, that way I shoot the bigger targets first to get a good wind call, and finish up with my last 6 shots on the smallest target. **10 rounds**

Speed drills:

5 targets on a rack, start prone mag in bolt back, engage each target with one shot each in 20 seconds, 1.5 MOA target size. **5 rounds**

Practice speed in conjunction with a target array shot near to far and back. Three targets sized at 2 MOA, 5 shots in 30 seconds, engage: near, middle, far, middle, near. You will use hold overs. **5 rounds**

Both these drills will help you learn to shoot without thinking about the fundamentals: trigger squeeze, cheek and shoulder pressure, bolt manipulation, breathing, should become second nature. If you have not mastered these fundamentals, you will struggle with these drills.

First stage nervousness:

This is a common problem. To help eliminate it, use your practice trips as a real match start. What I mean is rather than do your normal routine of shooting dope or zero, have a buddy run you through a stage. Cold bore/cold shooter under time constraints. That is what happens in a match, why would you not practice it? **10 rounds**

13 Rifle Precision

We all strive to achieve the maximum amount of precision from our rifles for any type of shooting we are involved in. Whether it is shooting prairie dogs, hunting in the mountains, or competing, an accurate rifle and load benefits in all of these endeavors. Different users have very different requirements.

The typical F-Class shooter is held to much tighter accuracy and precision requirements to be competitive/effective than the average hunter, as well as someone participating in the precision rifle competitions that are popping up all over the country. Shooting small, distant targets undoubtedly becomes easier with a precise rifle. While multiple impacts can still be made with rifles that shoot 1 MOA, adjusting rounds onto target can become frustrating and misleading. A properly-tuned load makes precise adjustments easier and more accurate, provided the wind stays the same, and the shooter does his/her part.

I sometimes hear competitors at a precision rifle match claim that their .25 MOA rifle is opening up to .5 MOA, and they are now thinking of trashing the barrel soon. Personally, I think this is a bit ridiculous. A .5 MOA rifle is more than adequate to compete in most precision rifle arenas. Quite honestly, a 1 MOA rifle will suit most people's needs; what makes the difference is the size of the targets being engaged.

Everyone has different accuracy requirements for their rifle. For me, I like to stay around .5 MOA. If I get better than that, great! If not, I don't bother trying to develop the load further and chase the purple dragon into oblivion, wasting both my time and ammunition. For positional shooting, .5 MOA will suffice since the VAST majority of misses will be due to bad shots and wind calls (aka, us!). However, through my experiences, I know that I can still place fairly well with a .75 MOA rifle.

A .75 MOA rifle isn't ideal, but the average size of targets found in these matches is around 2-3 MOA, so I don't sweat it too much. I have competed in a few national-level matches with a rifle that was shooting .75 MOA for various reasons (most of them my fault) and have come away with a 7th place, 8th place, and tie for 3rd place finish. Upon review of each match (the shoulda-coulda-woulda period), I determined that "if" I had avoided the problem and had a .5 MOA or better load, I would have moved no more than a maximum of 1 or maybe 2 places up. As I stated before, taking the time to break good shots and make good wind adjustments will be infinitely more beneficial to your scores/hit percentages than chasing that last tiny bit of precision.

Where the extra precision does help (.5 MOA and below) is with the uncertainty factor and, of course, very small targets. With a .5 MOA or better rifle, if the round impacts closer to the bottom of the target you know that a small adjustment up is needed since your rifle has a smaller cone of dispersion. If the rifle's precision was worse, at around 1-2 MOA, your drop data/zero could be dead on, but you would possibly have impacts high and low on the target. This could lead to a bad correction and cause more frustration. Shooters often only have a maximum of one shot to make a correction. Knowing the shot went where it was supposed to increases confidence in accurate and correct adjustments.

Improved precision also shows its worth on shots that break closer to the edge of the target than we like. Suppose that we are shooting a 2 MOA target from a less than stable position. With a 1 MOA rifle/load, not very much movement is required before the cone of dispersion starts falling off the target. A .5 MOA rifle lets the shooter get away with more error in shot placement, assuming everything else is done correctly: trigger press, no scope shadow, no parallax, etc.

Below, I have scaled images representing the effect precision has on impacting a 2 MOA target. For positional considerations, especially at distance, this is a fairly small target. Each aiming point is placed as far as possible from the center before the cone of dispersion starts to fall off the edge of the target. The wind is obviously not factored in. The large circle represents the target, the small circle is the rifle's cone of dispersion, and the cross is the aiming point in the center of the cone.

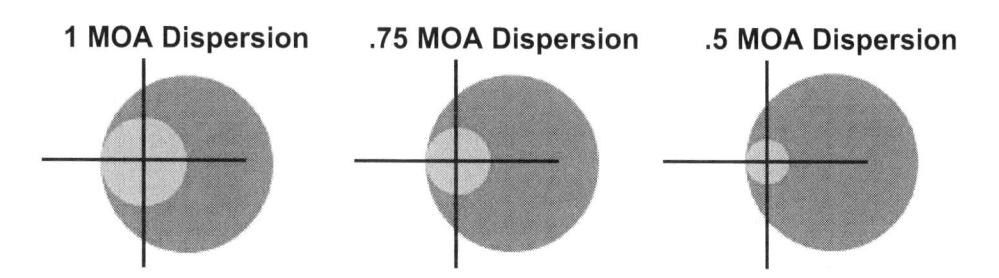

1 MOA Dispersion　　　**.75 MOA Dispersion**　　　**.5 MOA Dispersion**

As you can see, the person shooting the 1 MOA rifle/load has to be more careful in where they break that shot to achieve a 100 percent chance of impacting the target when compared to the .5 or .75 MOA rifle/load. Again, wind is not factored in, and we are assuming the fundamentals are being properly executed. This is also a very rudimentary representation of the issue. At longer distances, the wind wreaks havoc on the horizontal plane. Variations in muzzle velocity can also cause the dispersion to fall outside these parameters, depending on how well your ammunition's standard deviation is.

Unless you are in the running for a Top 3 or Top 5 ranking in large precision rifle matches, a .75 or even 1 MOA rifle will be able to do most everything you ask of it. Once you reach the higher level of competition is where the .5 MOA and better rifle will become a necessity. A couple of points are often all that separates 1st place from 5th place and shooters need all the additional hits they can get. Because if we are all honest with ourselves, we don't break all our shots perfectly in the middle every single time when we are shooting from an obstacle. A shooter with a 1 MOA rifle/load who is solid in their positional shooting will outperform the shooter with the .25 MOA rifle/load that can't shoot well from positions other than their belly.

For the hunters out there, consider the fact that the vital zone of the average whitetail deer is around 10 inches. I will not get into the argument over long-range hunting, but realize that 10 inches becomes relatively small very quickly. If the deer is at 500 yards, this represents an effective target area of just under 2 MOA. If you are in a position with even a little wobble and have a 1-2 MOA rifle, your margin of error in your wobble is just about zero.

Include any wind or ranging errors and your chances of a clean impact are reduced even further. The benefits of more precise rifles/loads can clearly be seen in this example. Even if the animal is much closer, knowing your round will go precisely where it is aimed helps put the mind at ease in the moments before the shot.

In the end, we are always the weakest link in the rifle's system, so we should strive to improve our shooting from every position first to more effectively place rounds on target.

14 Firing Through Brush

It is common knowledge that shooting through tree branches and other thick mediums will have adverse effects on the trajectory of the bullet. Multiple tests have been done to prove this. It is best to avoid these situations as much as possible. On the other side of the flora density spectrum, we have grass and light brush found out in the field. I've always been told to avoid firing through these as well. I found this to be curious since I could think back to multiple situations where I had shot through grass and brush tops that partially, or completely, obscured the target from various distances and still hit the intended target.

Remember that this test is for one caliber (6.5mm) with hollow point boat tail match bullets. I highly encourage you to test this yourself with your given caliber and projectile.

I decided to test this for myself and get a more definitive answer than what the internet gurus could type up. The test was conducted by engaging a target (red circle is approximately 2.5" in diameter) from prone at 405 yards with the test brush set 1.5 - 2 feet in front of the muzzle. The brush was placed in a container more effectively to control the density and height of the medium. I chose ~400 yards because it was a long enough range that any signs of deflection could be easily seen, while a short enough range that the effects of light wind and muzzle velocity variations wouldn't be too pronounced. Shots taken while hunting often fall within this range (area dependent).

After each shot, I would get up to rearrange and rotate the brush ensuring the muzzle was lined up properly with an area of the brush. To keep everything as consistent as possible, I broke my position and got up to walk around in between each shot while shooting the control groups as well. Once I built another prone position, I would dry fire one to three times to confirm I had a good natural point of aim, and I was mentally ready for the next shot. This was repeated for each of the 5 shots in each category. No adjustments to the scope were made throughout the test. The On Target Precision Calculator software was used to analyze group sizes and was confirmed with caliper measurements on the actual target.

This test was done twice, on separate days, at temperatures between 70 - 75 degrees and a density altitude reading of 6800 - 7000 feet. I should also note that I ran out of the lot of powder used in the first test before I could complete the second test. The load was worked back up to match the velocity (~2820 fps) with a new lot of powder. The precision measured across multiple groups with the new lot of powder before the second test was in the vicinity of .4 - .55 MOA, so slightly larger on average than the old lot of powder which was around .35 MOA.

Test #1

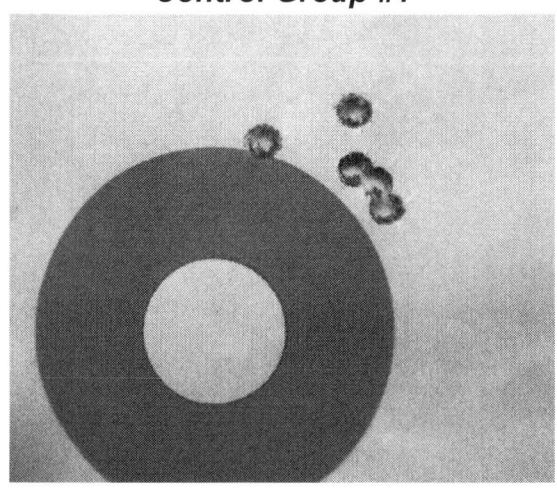

Control Group #1

Onto the first test: Dried up field grass. The density of the grass used may have been a little higher than one would find lying in a field, but I wanted to ensure that the bullet would contact the grass on every shot. The muzzle blast would blow over a good portion of the grass during each shot, so additional grass was periodically added to keep the density roughly equal to when I started. The first 5-round group shot through the grass measured at 2.594", or .612 MOA, with most of the dispersion being vertical. As I stated before with this older lot of powder, I would *typically* see groups average around .35 MOA, so it does appear that the grass could have had an effect on the trajectory of the rounds. I expected to see more horizontal deflection, not vertical. Maximum width of this group was 1.033" and the vertical was 2.503".

Grass Test #1

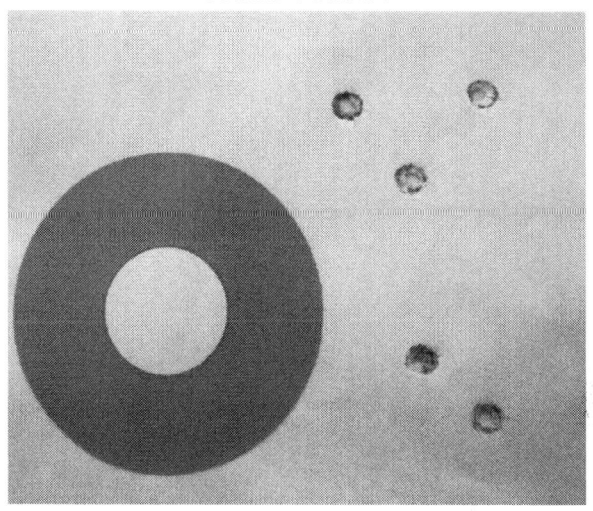

For the other brush that was tested, I decided to use sage tops. Only the tops though, since the thicker branches would obviously deflect the bullet and the tops are more likely to be shot through when building an elevated position. Muzzle blast didn't disrupt the sage tops as much as the grass, but care was still taken to set up the sage in the same way each time.

I was surprised at the results on this first sage test. The groups landed in nearly the same place as the control and just ever so slightly to the right. Group size measured at .375 MOA, hardly a discernible difference from the control. When I observed the group through the scope, I was worried that all the bullets had somehow missed any part of the sage.

Sage Test #1

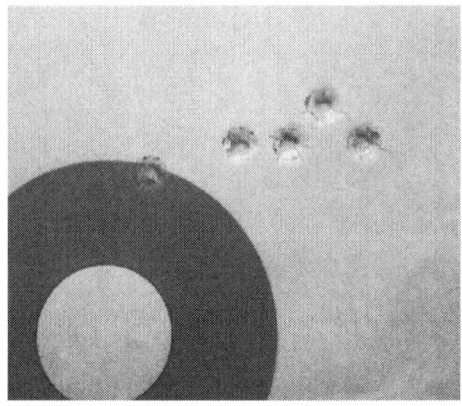

Upon inspection of the target, it was clear that the bullets made contact with both the grass and the sage. The black ring of carbon that is usually present on paper when bullets pass through was noticeably less pronounced on the grass target. The bullets that had been shot through the sage left almost no carbon ring on the paper at all!

Once I had completed these first tests, I decided to double the density of the grass just to see what the results would be through an extremely dense cluster of grass. Each bullet passed through about 3 inches of constant contact with the grass. I realize that finding and firing through grass this thick is not exactly realistic, but was just curious what the results would be. In the picture below, the extremely thick cluster of grass clearly had a negative effect on the trajectory.

Extremely Thick Grass During Test #1

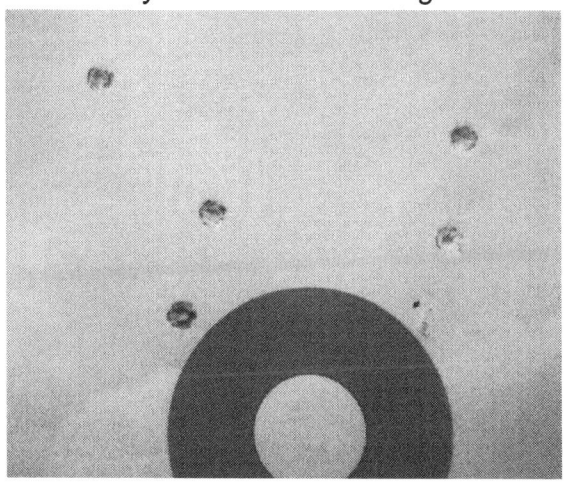

Firing through this density of grass increased the group size by nearly 2.5 times from the .35 MOA average. The center of the group shifted about 1.55", or around .37 MOA up and to the left from the control. No wind gusts were observed during the firing of this group and no visible changes in mirage. There was a very small amount of mirage present during the first outing, but not enough to distort the target image.

Test #2

I wanted to see if these results could be somewhat duplicated, but I wasn't sure due to the randomness of brush. Test #2 was conducted in the same manner as Test #1 with the new lot of powder and reworked load. While firing the second control group, there was some slight right to left mirage but no observed wind above 1-2 mph at the firing position. The horizontal in the group may have been due to trace amounts of wind downrange, or very well could have been me. Nevertheless, the group was left as-is and was not reshot to maintain consistency between tests.

Control Group #2

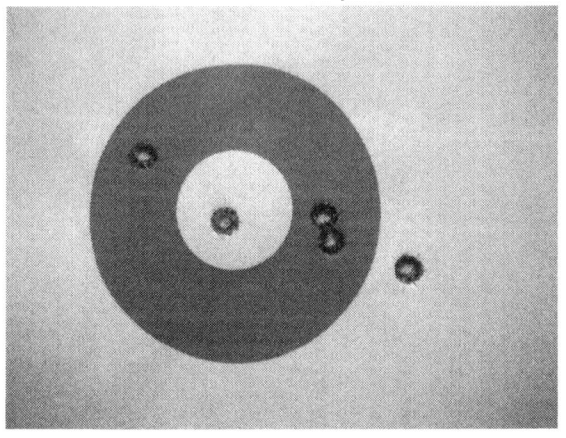

I was expecting the second grass test to follow a similar pattern as the first and was surprised to see a round, 1.238" (.292 MOA) group appear. The group had shifted 1.65" down and to the right. I suspect the no-wind zero of the control group was around the three shots clustered on the right, but the grass still showed a very slight shift to the right if that were the case.

Grass Test #2

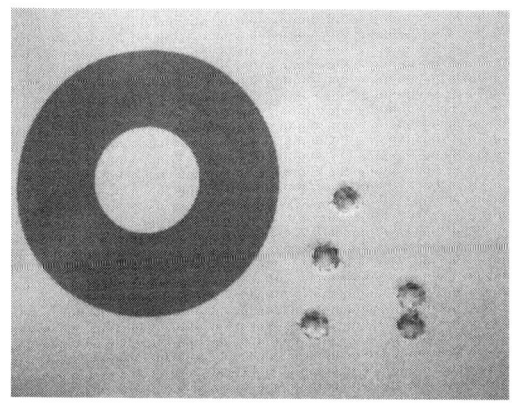

The results from the second sage test mimicked the grass test from the first day. The group remained slightly right from the control but was strung vertically. Overall group size was 2.644" (.624 MOA) with 2.631" of vertical and .477" horizontal dispersion. I would need to have extreme muzzle velocity variations to see this sort of spread, and this ammunition typically stays within a 20 fps extreme spread. This will account for approximately half an inch at this distance, so it's clearly the brush acting upon the bullet.

Sage Test #2

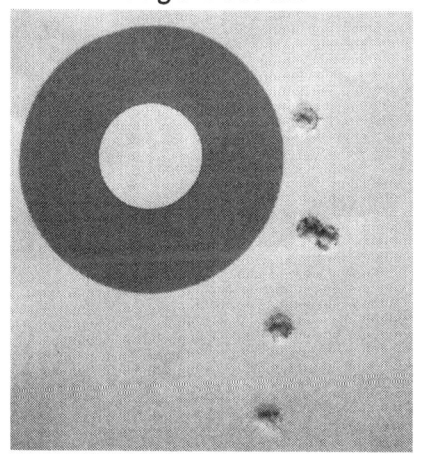

Below, I have a table with the overall results of the five round groups fired through each medium in both tests that were repeated.

	Control	Grass	Sage Tops
Test #1 Group Size	.226 MOA	.612 MOA	.375 MOA
Test #2 Group Size	.579 MOA	.292 MOA	.624 MOA
Average Group Size	.403 MOA	.452 MOA	.500 MOA

Practical Takeaways

While this test is far from scientific, I believe that the results gave enough evidence for me to stop. I expected more horizontal deflection to occur rather than vertical. As we can see, any measurable amount of bullet deflection was hard to repeat between mediums and oddly enough mostly vertical, except the single test with extremely thick grass. That group remained fairly rounded but much larger than the others.

Even though there was evidence of very slight POI shift in some cases and some reason to believe that firing through sage tops and thick grass slightly increased group size, I don't think this will deter me from occasionally firing through field grass. If I were shooting at a steel target in a match or the vital zone of a deer at this range, I wouldn't hesitate to take the shot.

I placed an 8" circle over the center of each one of the targets' aiming points and despite having an imperfect zero, 100% (25/25) of the shots through brush would have impacted within that circle (~2 MOA). With a 4" circle (~1 MOA) over the aiming point, 56% (14/25) of the shots would have impacted within the circle. The hit percentage for the 4" circle would have been dramatically increased if I had corrected my zero to the left, but I didn't change it to maintain consistency between tests. This includes both days of testing and the one test that had the extremely thick grass. Again, note that this is one set of tests that most likely won't prove true for all rifle setups and situations. Firing a bullet through a stretch of grass 15-20 feet long will most likely have different results than 3" of grass at the muzzle.

As you can see, the size of the target you are engaging from behind brush should also be taken into consideration. If the target is smaller, around 1 MOA, then try to stay out of very thick grass and brush. If the target is larger (2 MOA or more), this opens up a much larger margin of error for the bullet to still make an impact. You know your rifle and load better than anyone else, so the final judgement remains with you.

I can say that for my caliber/bullet/rifle combination (6.5mm Creedmoor/139 Scenar/roughly .5 MOA and under rifle), the overall effects of light grass and brush are minimal. This confirms my previous experiences of firing through sage tops and light field grass during matches and other outings. While I think I would choose to find a better position if I were shooting 1000+ yards through thick grass, I don't consider sparse grass an obstacle worth considering for practical purposes.

Grass Testing

Sage Testing

15 Summary

While many of my examples stem from the competition world, realize that positional shooting is positional shooting, regardless of where you are. Barricades and tank traps can easily be replaced with fence lines, boulders, and trees; the principles remain the same.

1 - Support the front of the rifle
2 - Support the rear of the rifle, or the elbow
3 - Get as low as is comfortable

Use this guide book as a starting point for your positional shooting and future training sessions. As I have stressed throughout the book, there are many different ways of tackling problems; no single way works best for each person. Arguing on the internet over techniques and gear used is easy but does not progress anyone's shooting ability. Be the one that dedicates the time to develop a structured and consistent dry-fire regimen. Make every round and repetition count during practice. Cultivate a mentality of verifying the things you hear on the range and read on the internet. There is a lot of good information out there, but it must be sorted through and confirmed for yourself before it can be treated as a truth.

Remember that while reading books and watching videos will help you gain valuable knowledge, make sure you dry fire and get out to the range in order to apply and engrain the principles! Reading all the books ever written on shooting will never replace actual time on the gun. Constantly question techniques to see how, and why, they work so you may find which method is best for you. The amount of progression the precision rifle world has seen even within the last five years is incredible, in both equipment and shooter ability. None of this progress would have been made if it was not for shooters and companies questioning the status quo and pushing the boundaries of what was traditionally considered possible.

I hope this guide book will benefit you in whatever shooting endeavor you are in, whether it is competition, recreation, hunting, or anything else. I promise that if you apply these principles and dedicate time to quality dry-fire practice, you will see an improvement in your shooting from any position.

About the Author

Marcus Blanchard grew up in Henderson, Nevada and St. George, Utah, where he learned to shoot from his father and began competing in NRA Service Rifle and precision rifle matches. Upon graduating high school, he enlisted in the Marine Corps and served as an 0313 Light Armored Vehicle Crewman with 3rd Light Armored Reconnaissance Battalion (2009-2013) on deployments to Helmand Province, Afghanistan, and Okinawa, Japan.

During his time in the Marine Corps, Marcus traveled to Las Vegas, NV and Phoenix, AZ on his available weekends to compete with the clubs that hosted precision rifle matches. It was at these matches and clubs that Marcus built a strong base to start competing in the emerging Precision Rifle Series. There, he has gone on to win the 2016 New Mexico Precision Rifleman's Championship, and regularly place in the top 5 or top 10 in nearly every national match he has competed in. Marcus also finished 8th overall for the 2015 Precision Rifle Series national ranking. In addition to being a regular competitor, Marcus also is on staff at Deliberate Dynamics Inc. (DDI) as a precision rifle instructor.

Marcus currently lives in Utah where he is pursuing a Bachelor of Science in Finance from Utah Valley University.

Printed in Great Britain
by Amazon